Your Life Story
By
Shawn A O'Neil

This book was written with care and heart.
Please don't copy or share it without asking.
Copyright © 2025 by Shawn A. O'Neil
ISBN: 978-0-9718714-5-8
Published by Palindromist Press

Many Thanks

One of the stories in this book, *The Leather Shop*, played a key role in inspiring cover design. While the standard editions of this book do not feature it, I may create special editions with a handcrafted leather cover by Elaine Waters, the owner of Uisce Saddlery Leather Workshop. If you ever find yourself in Dingle, Ireland, stop by Uisce Saddlery Leather Workshop, give the dogs a pat, and say hello to Elaine. I'm sure you'll agree that her craftsmanship is of the highest caliber.

I cannot say enough about my good friend and editor, Gregor Clark. He is a man with many *Scèal Do Bheatha*, having traveled all over the world as a writer for *Lonely Planet*—yes, those invaluable guides you rely on when you travel! His talent and insight were of the greatest value to me.

Thanks to Terry Simpkins for his guidance on copyright matters.

I must also thank everyone who has inspired me to write these short snippets of my life. Many of you are in these stories—after all, I wouldn't have stories without you. My dad was a huge influence on my love for storytelling. Thanks, Dad! I'm sure you're still telling stories in the great beyond.

This journal is dedicated to my children, Fiona, Riley, and Finn. I hope these small glimpses into their dad's life are passed down to future generations.

Thanks

Shaun

INTRODUCTION

This is my story, your story, our story. This is *Scèal Do Bheatha* (Your Life Story). We all have our own personal stories in life. Each of us is a unique individual, shaped by different experiences and perspectives on our journey. The book you hold in your hands contains some of my brief *scèals*—stories I freely share with you. My hope is that as you read these glimpses into my life, they will spark memories or *scèals* of your own. While our experiences may be different, we all have stories worth telling.

I have formatted this book as a journal, with empty pages following my stories. My intention is for my stories to serve as a catalyst for your own. If they spark a memory, you now have space to capture it. Write, draw, calculate—whatever feels right. Those blank pages are yours.

This project began many years ago when I started sending jokes, puns, or quotes to a few coworkers every Friday, something to make them smile (or groan) at the end of a long week.

Then, in 2020, the COVID-19 pandemic changed the world. Many people were working from home, and uncertainty was everywhere. I decided it was time to "up my game." I started adding short stories to my *Pundays*, and soon, the format evolved into *Happy Punday and a Short Story*. Each entry included a brief introduction, a joke or quote, and a short personal story—sometimes with accompanying photos. My goal was to write something that would spark a similar memory in my readers. To reach a wider audience, I began sharing my stories on Facebook as well.

I made it a habit to write *Punday and a Short Story* every Friday, though I occasionally missed a week or wrote my story on the same day. I was surprised by how many memories I could pull from my past, and I kept a list to avoid repeating the same stories.

The idea for this book's format and cover logo came to me during my morning meditation. As soon as I finished, I had a clear vision of the book's structure and quickly wrote it down before I could forget. While jotting down my thoughts, the logo also came to me—a Celtic symbol of the Tree of Life alongside the words *Life Story*. Since the symbol was Celtic, I felt the words should be in Irish. Using Google Translate, I found *Scèal Do Bheatha*, which fit perfectly.

My hope for you, the reader, is that this book brings to mind the happy, exciting, and memorable moments in your own life. Each of us is unique, and every life holds a story worth telling. We all have *Scèal Do Bheatha*.

Table of Contents

Family and Friends

A day with Janida 1

Autumn in Vermont 5

    Bailey 9

  Google Girl 14

  Tim and I 18

The Fairy Cottage 23

The Chipmunk Whisperer 27

Smiley Riley and Violet 32

  Randy Rice 36

  Kids' Births 41

   Henry 45

Fiddlehead Kitty 49

  Big Cathy 53

  Band-aid 57

Aunt Renee 61

  Uncle Billy 66

The Dynamic Dou 70

The Dog Chase 75

Nite Nite Bear 79

Guenhwyvar 84

The Flip phone 88
Elderly Care 92
George and Peg 96

Childhood and Young Adult

The Little Redhouse on Glen Street 102
The Dark Road 107
Rainy Days 112
Moving Out 116
Morning Run 120
Halloween 124
The Swimming Quarry 128
The Projectionist 132
The Mine 136
I had my Lady as a boy 140
Winter Cave 144
Trust Me 148
The Huffy 152
The Cow Field 156
Siblings did the most stupid things 160
Poison Ivy 164
New Year's Traditions 168
Falling and flying 172

Traveling and Strangers

- The Wishing Well 178
- The Waving Man 182
- The Video Return 186
- The Leather Shop 190
  - Route One 194
  - Fog 198
  - Driving on the left! 202
  - Traveling with strangers 206
  - Abba and Donegal 210
  - The Emerald Isle 214
  - The Carrygerry House 219
  - Strangers and Friends 224
- Sea Caves 228

Family and Friends

"There are friends, there's family, and then there are friends that become family"
Unknown

A day with Janida

You meet so many people throughout your life. Some pass through briefly, while others linger and touch your heart. This is the story of an elderly woman who became one of the latter in my life.

"Dying is a wild night and a new road" Emily Dickinson

The sun shone brightly through the greenhouse windows, casting a golden light around us. The vibrant purple and red flowers glowed in the sunlight, their colors even more vivid in the warmth of the day. We stood there in silence, simply taking in the beauty of the moment.

I had brought my elderly companion to this little sanctuary, nestled on the sixth floor of the science building where I worked. I knew she would love this small paradise. Earlier, we visited the college museum, exploring an exhibit of photographs spanning all ages. We even stepped into the photo booth together, taking a picture and pinning it to the bulletin board alongside all the others—a memory captured in time.

It was a day of adventure. We started with brunch at Rosie's, then drove around the campus, stopping at various spots to take in the scenery. Finally, we returned to the house where she lived with her daughter and her family, my good friends.

But when we got back, she realized her purse was missing. We searched the house, turning over cushions, retracing our steps, but it was nowhere to be found. I called Rosie's, hoping it had been left behind, but they hadn't seen it. Determined to find it, I backtracked our entire day, checking every place we had visited. Still, no luck.

When I finally returned to the house, feeling defeated, she met me at the door with an impish, slightly embarrassed smile. In her hands, she held the missing purse.
"I found it," she admitted. "It was hanging on the back of my rocker."

I sighed with relief, and we both burst into laughter. The rest of the evening was spent watching her favorite TV show *Gunsmoke* and anything related to the Old West.

Janida grew up on the Great Plains, and she had incredible stories of the past. She was an educated woman, and when her husband passed unexpectedly and far too soon, she raised her children as a single mother.

Her passing will be felt deeply by many, but her legacy will live on in her children and grandchildren. I am honored to have been considered her friend and to have been a witness to her life.

Do you have an elderly friend?

Autumn in Vermont

Autumn in Vermont is my favorite season. It is a piece of heaven brought down to earth.

"All in all, Vermont is a jewel state, small but precious." Pearl S. Buck

"It was a beautiful bright autumn day, with air like cider and a sky so blue you could drown in it." Diana Gabaldon, Outlander

The sun shone brightly, and the air was crisp and sharp. I closed my eyes, lifted my head, and let the warmth of the sun wash over my face. Behind my closed eyelids, the darkness brightened slightly. The earthy aroma of fallen leaves mixed with the slightly sweet scent of apples filled the air. When I opened my eyes, I watched golden sun rays filter through the branches of an apple tree.

My three kids eagerly reached for the lower branches, plucking apples and placing them into the paper tote bags they lugged by their sides.

"Dad! Look at that one up there," my youngest called out. "Can you get it?" I stretched, reaching for the big red apple that had caught his attention. "Dad, do you think we'll find the wooden apple?" my oldest asked excitedly.

This orchard had a tradition—they hid a special wooden apple somewhere among the countless trees. Whoever found it would win an Apple computer.

"I don't know," I said with a smile. "But I don't think anyone has found it yet. Maybe you'll be the lucky one."

She grinned and studied every apple carefully, her hands moving through the branches with determined focus.

Beside her, my middle child followed closely, helping with the search. At this age, she was like her sister's shadow.

It was autumn in Vermont—apple picking, leaf raking, and jumping into the giant piles of leaves we had just gathered.

The landscape transformed into a breathtaking patchwork of reds, oranges, and golds. Cars with out-of-state license plates slowly patrolled Vermont's back roads, their drivers searching for the perfect scene to capture. They pulled over at random, sometimes in the most inconvenient spots, eager to bring home a piece of this fleeting beauty to their concrete cities.

What are your memories of Autumn?

Bailey

Bailey was a Christmas gift for my kids—a medium-sized, short-haired white dog with black spots who was about to become part of our family.

"I think having an animal in your life makes you a better human." Rachael Ray, American Television Personality (Her dogfood brand is Bailey's favorite)

"Until one has loved an animal, a part of one's soul remains unawakened." Anatole France, French Poet

She had a bright red Christmas bow on her collar when I surprised my son. The girls had known ahead of time, but we all wanted to make it a special surprise for him. My oldest and I had gone to the animal shelter earlier that day to prepare Bailey for her big moment.

My middle daughter had the important job of bringing him to the shelter. She made up an excuse, telling him she needed to pick up a "friend "which wasn't exactly a lie. When they arrived, the look on his face was priceless. His excitement bubbled over as he kept repeating, *"We got a dog!"*

Bailey was just as thrilled to be with her new family. But I was a little worried at first, I noticed she could be too aggressive toward new people and other dogs. I knew it often took time for animals to adjust to new surroundings, so I hoped she would settle in.

A few weeks later, I started to see a change in her. She was still cautious around strangers and other dogs, but she was adjusting. My middle daughter took the lead in helping her, bringing Bailey on hikes and long walks. She had plenty of space to run freely in the open fields around our home, and the more freedom she had, the better she became. She was an incredibly smart dog, and if she could have spent all day chasing balls, she would have. Bailey was also fiercely protective of her new family. I never worried when my kids went for nighttime walks with her, I knew she would never let anything happen to them.

At home, she was the cuddliest companion. Every morning, I'd sit in my chair with a cup of coffee, and Bailey would jump up and curl up beside me. On lazy weekends, we sometimes even dozed off like that together.

A year later, I learned more about Bailey's past. She once belonged to a loving family, but they lived in a small apartment with teenagers and other dogs. She spent most of her time crated, hardly getting the chance to stretch her legs. She probably had to compete for both attention and food.

Suddenly, it all made sense why she embraced her freedom so fully, why she ran with such pure joy. She seemed to understand that as long as she listened to us, her freedom would never be taken away. She obeyed, not out of fear, but because she had learned to trust.

I also found out that we were Bailey's third family. The shelter had a three-strike policy: if a dog was deemed too aggressive and failed to adjust with multiple owners, they would be put down. Bailey had already been through two homes. We saved her.

Now, two years later, Bailey has come a long way. The people in our neighborhood are part of her pack, and she's much less aggressive with strangers. She's even learned to coexist with Bella, the big Lab next door, though she still lets Bella know when she's had enough. And when Bailey feels overwhelmed, she no longer lashes out. Instead, she comes to me or one of her people, knowing she's safe.

She has taught me that with enough love and freedom, any being can grow into something better.

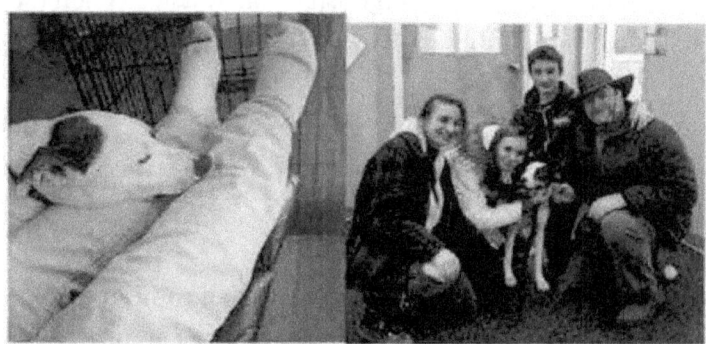

Did you have a special pet?

Google Girl

I've traveled alone and gotten lost before. But getting lost with someone else? That's a different experience altogether. With the right person, it can be an adventure. With the wrong person, it can be a nightmare.

"You are not regarded as lost until you realize you're lost!" - Mehmet Murat

"Google Maps tells me where to go, then recalculates to something else. It's like getting directions from a drunk friend in the back seat" Chris Rogers

Uncle Billy and I raced down a California highway in his Mercedes SLX Roadster, one of his many projects. We were taking it for a test ride, heading north to visit his brother—my Uncle Mike.

It was a typical sunny California day. We weaved through traffic, the wind rushing past us. I had entered Uncle Mike's address into my phone, relying on Google Maps. The Irish-accented female voice—whom we had affectionately named *Google Girl*—chimed in occasionally to guide us.

Uncle Billy had only been to his brother's new house once before, so we put our faith in Google Girl to lead the way.

We were deep in conversation when she suddenly announced, "Take the next exit." Trusting her guidance, we turned off the highway, still immersed in our discussion.

Our conversation came to an abrupt halt when we followed another turn and found ourselves in an industrial park. Grey, lifeless buildings surrounded us. Not a single person was in sight.

Had it gotten cloudy? Probably not, but looking back, the mood certainly felt overcast.

Google Girl had failed us. We were lost.

I re-entered Uncle Mike's address, determined to get back on track. We returned to the highway, followed the new directions... and ended up in the exact same place.

"What the...?" We both stared at each other, sitting in the middle of an empty parking lot.

For a brief moment, I wouldn't have been surprised if a gang suddenly appeared, forcing us to peel off in a dramatic escape. But, of course, that didn't happen. Instead, we both sighed, knowing what had to be done.

We called Uncle Mike.

And just like that, our charming Irish Google Girl was replaced by a grumpy, no-nonsense Massachusetts-accented Uncle Mike, who guided us—rather impatiently—to his house.

Have you ever been lost while traveling?

Tim and I

I grew up with four sisters. Luckily, I had male cousins close to my age to balance things out. We were bonded by both blood and camaraderie. Ronny and Timmy were the two closest to me in age, and I had countless adventures with each of them. Timmy, or Tim as he later preferred to be called, spent a lot of time with my sisters and me. He was like a younger brother to us.

"Having family around is the best feeling ever, but when you have cousins to grow up with, they are what help keep everything together." **anonymous**

"Family: a little bit of crazy, a little bit of loud, and a whole lot of love." **anonymous**

Together, we wandered the streets of Worcester on grand adventures, back in the days before cell phones, the internet, or any of the technologies that now keep people tethered. We had the whole city to explore—so long as we were back by dinner.

Our headquarters for these adventures was the third-story apartment where Uncle Mike, Aunt Bev, and Timmy lived. During the summers, I'd spend weekends there, and our explorations would begin.

We'd walk to a nearby restaurant, sit at the counter, and ask for a free glass of tap water. Other times, we'd head to the local drugstore to buy penny candy. But our favorite destination was *Toys R Us*, just a few blocks away. I still remember the excitement of getting my first X-Wing fighter there.

Beyond the city, there was another special place we all shared—our grandmother's house. Across from it stood Pine Forest and Foster's Pond, the same woods where our parents had once played as children. My sisters, Timmy, and I spent countless hours there, creating stories of our own.

One day, while Timmy, my sister Cathi, and I were playing near Foster's Pond, we made a surprising discovery. Beneath a massive bush that we had claimed as our fort, we unearthed a buried treasure—a machete. How it got there was a mystery. Excited but knowing it was, after all, a weapon, we turned it over to our parents. To this day, I have no idea what it became of.

As time passed, we all grew up, leaving childhood behind and stepping into the responsibilities of adulthood. Jobs, families, and life pulled us in different directions. We moved away from Pine Forest and Foster's Pond. The pond remained, but the forest was lost—replaced by houses, erasing the playground of generations before us.

Distance and time made staying in touch more difficult, but modern-day social media reconnected us. Tim was especially good at reaching out—calling or texting now and then, just to stay connected. I will miss those little moments. I miss him.

But I know he's off on new adventures. And perhaps, in some way, I'll still hear from him— whether in the scent of pine needles that stir a forgotten memory or in the echo of a familiar voice saying:

"Shawn, what you doing?"

What past loved one puts a smile on your face when you think of them?

The Fairy Cottage

One of the traits that I hope my kids keep as adults is their imagination and creativity. With my oldest, whose birthday is in May, I have no doubt she will. This short story is dedicated to her.

"Imagination is more important than knowledge. For knowledge is limited. Imagination encircles the world"- Albert Einstein

You're only given a little spark of madness. You must lose it! Robin Williams

"If you fall in love with the imagination, you understand that it is free spirit. It will go anywhere, and it can do anything" Alice Walker

The tiny stick-and-flower cottage was nestled beautifully in the small woods near our home. My daughter spent hours perfecting it, carefully placing each twig and petal just so. She wanted to make sure the fairies would like it. In the center of the cottage, she arranged a small bundle of berries, nuts, buttons, and other shiny treasures—there might even have been a piece of chocolate—gifts she thought the fairies would enjoy.

Every day, she would check on her creation. Then, one afternoon, she burst into the house, breathless with excitement.

"Daddy, Daddy! The fairies came!"

"Oh? How do you know?" I asked, amused.

"They took the gift I left them!" she said, eyes wide with wonder.

"Oh, really?" I replied with a knowing smile.

She grabbed my hand and tugged me outside, racing back to the fairy cottage. "See!" she pointed eagerly. Sure enough, the offerings were gone, which, of course, I secretly knew.

Seventeen years later, my little fairy architect is now graduating from college. She still loves running wild through the woods. I don't know if she still builds fairy cottages, but I wouldn't be surprised, while wandering the forests near her school, you stumbled upon one of her creations. Just be careful, don't take any of the gifts inside. You wouldn't want to incur the wrath of the fairies... unless, of course, you have an accord with them

Later this year, Fiona and I will be traveling to the land of the fairies. Perhaps we'll build a tiny cottage on Emerald Isle. I'm sure the fairies there would appreciate it.

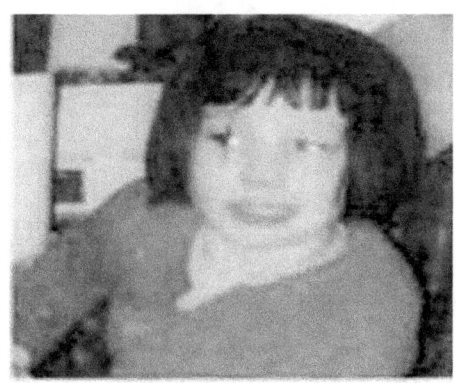

Do you have a childhood fantasy that you still believe in?

The Chipmunk Whisperer

Living in the country comes with its own unique set of "critter" situations. Here's one of them.

"The country is lyric, the town dramatic. When mingled, they make the most perfect musical drama." Henry Wadsworth Longfellow

Q: Why can't you be friends with a chipmunk? A: They drive everyone nuts.

I used to own a little red country house, and we had a cat that occasionally brought "gifts" inside. One day, the cat proudly trotted in with a chipmunk—very much alive. Mayhem erupted the moment the cat dropped its prize.

The tiny creature, who would soon earn the name Half-Tail (on account of its noticeably short tail), wasted no time making a break for it.

The cat lunged after the chipmunk. The dog chased the cat. The toddler chased the dog.

And I, the unfortunate dad in this situation, chased everyone.

From atop the kitchen table—where she had leaped in a single bound—my wife shrieked, "Get it! Get it!"

Chaos took over the living room.

Half-Tail bolted under the couch. The cat tried to follow, but the overexcited dog startled him, sending him scrambling onto the couch instead.

The toddler, caught up in the excitement, cheered, "No, Harley! Dadda, get mouse!"

"The chipmunk," I corrected, but no one was listening.

Knowing I was the only one in this house capable of handling wildlife, I managed to grab a pair of gloves mid-chase.

Peering under the couch, I found Half-Tail—his tiny chest heaving, eyes darting wildly for an escape. He bolted, but I was faster. With a careful but firm grip, I caught him.

He bit down, but the gloves were too thick for it to do any harm. The cat, perched on the couch, twitched his tail, ready to reclaim his prize. The dog barked excitedly. The toddler, in full toddler authority, scolded the dog. The wife remained on the table.

Cradling Half-Tail in my gloved hands, I spoke softly. "It's okay, little guy. It's okay." To my surprise, he stopped squirming. His breathing slowed. Even my wife looked on in amazement.

With the crisis under control, I headed outside. The cat slinked off, and the dog and toddler watched from the doorway as I walked up the sloping backyard to the stone wall. With one last reassuring pat, I released Half- Tail, who disappeared into the rocks.

Crisis averted. Or so I thought.

A week later, on a peaceful summer afternoon, I was outside while the dog and toddler played.

The cat was prowling near the stone wall. And then, down he came—Half-Tail in his mouth.

"You let Half-Tail go!" I shouted, exasperated. At my voice, the cat dropped Half-Tail, and the chase began again.

This time, however, something unexpected happened. Half-Tail, mid-sprint, heard my voice, changed course, and ran straight for me. Before I could react, the tiny chipmunk leaped onto my bare leg and clung for dear life.

Now, I'll admit—I screamed. But in a very manly way, of course.

Instinctively, I shook my leg, trying to dislodge my desperate little friend. Half-Tail had thought he was saved.

Instead, he was now airborne.

Disappointed but undeterred, the chipmunk hit the ground running, and the chase resumed. Like before, I was the first to reach him. Like before, I retrieved my gloves, calmed him down, and placed him safely back on the stone wall.

This time, as I stepped back, the dog, toddler, and cat stood at the bottom of the hill, watching silently as Half-Tail vanished once more into his stone fortress.

Would this be the last of Half-Tail's misadventures?

Have any critters ever run rampant in your house?

Smiley Riley and Violet

It is that time in my life when my kids are no longer kids; they have blossomed into adults. Somehow, it feels like it happened overnight. This is a short story about my middle daughter.

Absolutely, I don't believe in rules. As I tell my daughters when they are mischievous, "Well-behaved women rarely make history." Nia Vardalos.

"I hope that my daughters grow up empowered and don't define themselves by the way they look but rather by qualities that make them intelligent, strong, and responsible women." Unknown

We traveled all the way to a small town in New York state on a very specific mission: to "look" at some pug puppies. Of course, we all knew what "look" really meant.

Later that day, we headed back to Vermont with a tiny pug curled up in Riley's arms. I had been outvoted, and I dared not go against the majority.

A big smile stretched across Riley's face. She was Smiley Riley again. She had her pug.

Violet the pug—whose full name was much longer, though I can't remember it—became her constant companion. I just called her Violet.

Riley and Violet went everywhere together. She even took her on strolls around the neighborhood in a vintage golden pram stroller. People would coo at the "baby" inside, only to find a pug staring back at them, wide-eyed and content.

Riley and Violet shared a bond beyond words. They were kindred spirits.

Physically, they were opposites—Violet, short and squat, Riley, tall and slim. But their personalities? Uncannily similar. Both made people smile. Both were caring, protective, spunky, and full of life. They had a mischievous sense of humor, an adventurous spirit, and a natural ability to make friends wherever they went. People were drawn to them. They were fiercely loyal to their loved ones and, just as importantly, quick to forgive.

Oh, and they both loved cheese.

Now, Riley is off on her own, charting her own path. I have no doubt that her pug attitude will carry her far in life, bringing joy to everyone lucky enough to meet this bright, beautiful (inside and out) young woman.

Happy birthday, Sweetie. I love you, and I am so proud of you.

What memories do you think of when you think of pets and kids?

Randy Rice

It is always good to have a mentor in your life. By definition, a mentor is "a trusted counselor or guide." By that standard, parents can certainly be mentors, and throughout life, we are fortunate to have many. But I believe that having a mentor outside of family can be incredibly rewarding and deeply educational.

"Share your knowledge. It is a way to achieve immortality." Dalai Lama

"We must find time to stop and thank the people who make a difference in our lives." John F. Kennedy

I was sitting in my office when I heard that familiar voice:

"I'm looking for Shawn."

Before an introduction could even be made, I was already out of my chair, grinning as I greeted my friend, my mentor, and one of the finest human beings I've ever known.

"Randy!" I spoke. *"I'm glad you stopped by."*

We grabbed cups of coffee from the cart outside my workplace, took the elevator to the sixth floor, and entered my sanctuary—a lush, almost tropical greenhouse. Sunlight streamed through the glass, illuminating the vibrant greenery, while the gentle sound of a babbling brook filled the air. The warm aromas of earth and fresh foliage had a way of quieting even the busiest mind.

We sat at a metal table, drinking coffee and soaking in the beauty of the space.

Half-jokingly, we referred to this paradise as a "thin place" a place where the veil between this world and the eternal world is thin." It felt otherworldly, a sacred space where deep conversations came effortlessly. And with Randy Rice present, they always did.

Randy was a retired pastor, though as the saying goes, a pastor never truly retires. When I picture what a pastor should be, I see Randy.

An elderly man with a white beard and mustache, always wearing a smile and carrying a twinkle in his eyes. He had a dry wit, a huge heart, and an understanding of what it meant to be fully human.

Randy had an open mind and unwavering faith. His wisdom rivaled that of the Dalai Lama, shaped by both Eastern and Western experiences. He and his family had spent much of their lives in Korea as missionaries.

I cherished the times I spent with him.

When his wife was away visiting their kids and grandkids, we would have what we jokingly called a "bachelor's meal"—spaghetti, buttered bread, and some vegetables. Simple but meaningful.
Over dinner, we would talk about everything—faith, philosophy, life.

My dear friend, mentor, and pastor has now moved on. He is reunited with his beloved wife, who passed away a few years ago.

And yet, every time I step into my sixth-floor sanctuary, I still hear his voice—kind and full of wisdom. I see his broad smile, his twinkling eyes, and that unmistakable thin place clarity.

He will be missed but never forgotten.

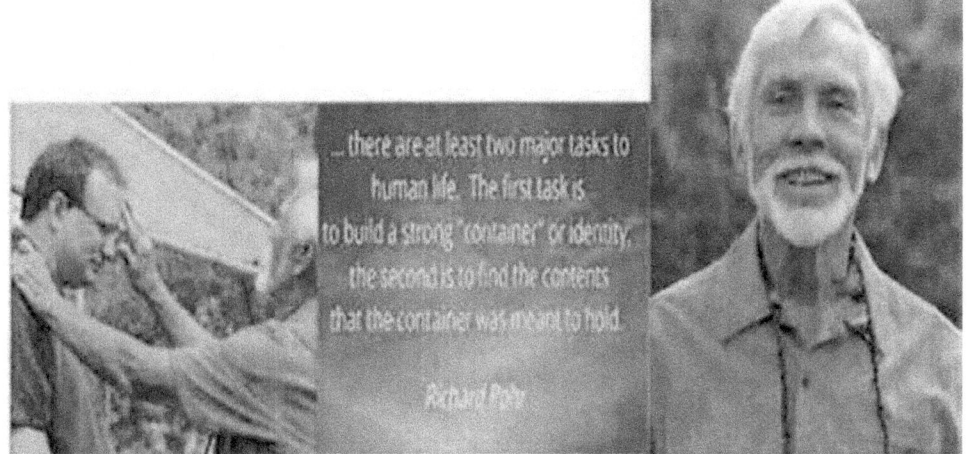

Who is your mentor?

kids' births

The last short story was about my dad and our relationship. It was about my memories and honoring him and his passing. I decided to go full circle and talk about new beginnings, births. So, this next story some of you have experienced in your own unique way.

What do you call a cow that's just given birth? Decalfinated

I remember all my three kids' births.

The first, Fiona's, happened the day I graduated from college on May 15th, 1999. I literally went from the hospital to my graduation.

The second, Riley's was two days after my birthday, November 5th, 2001, and we had just bought a new house.

The third and last was Finn, born on August 3rd, 2005—our one and only boy. His birth was different from the others—no meds, no drugs, just straight up natural.

Each one of my kids' births was unique and special to me. A memory that I will always remember and cherish.

Fiona: It was a nice warm May Day. This was our second time rushing to the hospital. I guess they have "false labor" as the doctor told us. I think it was because she was our first, so we were a little sensitive with the process. On May 15th at 12:12 midnight Fiona was born. I remember sleeping in the cot next to her and her mom. I can admit tears did leak out (on every one of my kids). I brought my graduation suit and gown and cap to the hospital. So, I kissed my baby girl goodbye and went to my college graduation. I was so tired at my graduation. The two people sitting next to me had to nudge me and prop me up during the ceremony. People may have thought I was drunk. Until they saw the writing on my cap, "It's A Girl". Now, my first will be graduating college next year!

Riley: We were between houses when Riley was born. We had a closing date of Nov. 7th. Riley was born on Nov. 6th at 3:05 pm. I guess it didn't matter to her that we had this process to go through. If anyone has ever bought a house, you know what I mean. Naturally the mother couldn't make it to the closing. Luckily, I found a nurse who was also a notary. We had to sign specific papers indicating that I would be the representative in this transaction. New baby, new home!

Finn: It was a hot summer day on August 3, 2005. Mom, mother In-law and dad were walking around the construction zone of the medical center in Burlington. About 20 minutes before that we were in a room full of nurses, doctors, and other people. All observing our friend inducing labor with acupuncture instead of drugs. This was a first for many people (including us). We had two nurses helping us. I fondly called them the older battle-worn nurse and the younger happy nurse.

The acupuncture really worked. It kicked in as we were walking through the construction zone heading for the delivery floor on the sixth floor. I raced ahead to warn the nurses and doctor. I raced into the delivery ward out of breath. It happened to be a shift change. So, the nurses there thought we were just coming in. Luckily the battle-worn nurse was still there, and she took control of the situation. At 5:55pm tears were running down my face as I looked from my baby boy into the crying eyes of my mother-in-law. We both laughed.

Do you remember your children's birth or witness a birth?

Henry

My sister got a call: "Don't panic! But I had to take Henry to the doctor's office. Something that a mom shouldn't hear when she is several thousand miles away in another state. Now, here are the "bloody" details that I am recalling from what I was told. This is from a third-party point of view so hopefully I will get the details correct:

"My nephew is my best mate in the world. He keeps me grounded and reminds me what life is all about." Steve Irwin (The Crocodile Hunter)

My young nephew (I think probably around 4 or 5) wanted an apple on the kitchen counter.
He got the apple. I guess he had it in his mind that he wanted to have only part of an apple. No one really knows what happened between this desire to have an apple and him going to the doctor's office (except perhaps Henry).

However, it may not take Sherlock Holmes to determine what happened after witnessing the scene of the crime.

Which was this: the apple had multiple punctured wounds, there was a little blood on the counter, most likely from the culprit. Various weapons were scattered around the crime scene, including a big knife, a small paring knife, a fork, a spoon, and a nail file, the latter of which I think was still plunged into the victim.

Now, this gruesome scene only took several minutes. The end results were that Henry had to get a stitch (I think), and he never got a piece of the apple.

Henry still has the determination to accomplish his goals. Fortunately, his inquisitive and creative mind has moved from trying to get a piece of an apple to facing and conquering challenges in his life. He is a handsome guy, talented artist, smart person, and an incredible athlete. He is the type of guy who you want to hang out with because of his positive, loving attitude.

I am proud to be Henry's uncle. Henry may have to go to the doctors occasionally. However, no matter what the challenge is he will be facing it with that determination, cleverness, and bravery. I also want him to know that Uncle Shawn will be cheering and encouraging him the whole way.

Love you, Henry -Uncle Shawn

Do you recall any younger relatives and their accomplishments?

Fiddlehead Kitty

Around this time of the year if you drive down the country dirt roads of Vermont you may see these curly ferns spread out on the forest floors. These are fiddleheads. The going rate for these is $11 a pound, which is about 100 to 150 fiddleheads. So, if you have the time, know the places to go and have the stamina to pick these, you could make some money and have some delicious fiddleheads.

What's Irish and comes out in Spring? Paddy O'Furniture Does February like Morch? No, but April Moy

If you were driving down the back roads of Vermont in the 1980s during spring, you might have seen an O'Neil's Appliance van parked off in the middle of nowhere. Going past the van you would have seen the owner wearing his appliance outfit and a little old white-haired lady, each holding bags and picking these little curly ferns.

My Dad and his mother, Grandma O'Neil, were expert and fanatical fiddlehead pickers. Just before the fiddlehead season my dad would know where all the best fiddleheads would be sprouting up. Since he drove all over the place fixing appliances, he would make sure to note where the best places were. He would report back to his mother. At the peak of fiddle head season Grandma O'Neil (she also got the nickname "Fiddlehead Kitty") would "go to work" with her son. The day would be a long one here because in between fixing appliances they would make stops to pick several bags of fiddleheads.

Nothing is more humbling than getting out picked by a 70-year-old woman. My Grandma could out pick anyone when it came to fiddleheads. I would proudly show that I got one bag full, only to turn around to see my grandma working on her third bag.

If my grandma were alive today, she would be awful rich from fiddleheads.

Do you have any memories of your grandparents?

Big Cathy

My family is slowly growing up, leaving home, and becoming adults. These life changes make me think back to when I was a kid and teen. One of the important influences in my life was Cathy, my stepmom (who I considered my "teen hood" mom).

"Families are like fudge - mostly sweet with a few nuts."-Les Dawson

"Family Isn't always blood. It's the people in your life who want you In theirs; the ones who accept you for who you are. The ones that would do anything to see you smile and who love you no matter what."-anonymous

The car ran outside the house. Cathy sat in it listening to her books on CD. She was totally oblivious to my dad frantically waving and yelling at her from the house window. He suddenly looked away from the window, mouthed some words, and disappeared from the window. He returned with a squirming, giggling little escape artist, baby girl, Fiona! The words mouthing "Will you hurry up!"

Shortly, Cathy came into the house greeted by a crawling Fiona. She picked her up and hugged her and walked into the disarranged living room. Toys, blocks, and all sorts of stuff were scattered around. There was a bin turned over with toys flowing from it. Cathy's husband, Fiona's grandpa, lay exhausted in his chair, glaring at her. "Didn't you see me at the window? What took you so long!"

"I was at a good part in my book. I had to finish it," she said while looking around. "I see you had a good time with Fiona?"

He just glared at her. "I didn't think someone so small could move so fast." She dumps everything! I couldn't keep up!" he said, "I would place her down, turn my head. And she would be across the room."

Cathy placed Fiona down. Fiona crawled to her grandpa who picked her up and placed her on his lap. Everything was good now.

Grandma was here. "Big Cathy" was given that name not because she was big but because my sister's name was Cathi, so the nickname helped distinguish the two. They each inherited "Big Cathy" and "Little Cathi" while they were in the same room together or you had to explain about which Cathy you were talking. Big Cathy was a big part of my life. Although she wasn't my biological mother, she was indeed a mother to me. I could proudly say I had two mothers. My biological mother raised me in my youth and Cathy raised me in my teenage years. They both were influential women in my life.

Are there any funny memories of your parents?

Band-aid

Life can bring joy and pain. Have you ever had one of these feelings and at first you do not understand why? One could analyze your situation and encounters to determine why.

Regardless of what the outcome is, you either deal with it or not. Sometimes dealing with the pain is just putting a band-aid on it to cover the wound to help it heal. The joy would be when you take that band-aid off and see that you are healed.

However, sometimes people keep the band-aid on even when they are healed.

My daughter screeched, "Daaaaad, you haven't listened to one word I've said, have you/?" What a strange way to start a conversation with me... anonymous

I was watching Star Wars with my daughter. She asked why Luke was climbing inside a Tauntaun, I said to keep warm. She asked how warm? I said lukewarm. anonymous

She had a band-aid on the middle of her 4-year-old brow. Riley, my daughter, needed a band-aid on her brow. I don't even know if she even had a wound there. However, she insisted that it be put there. That band-aid stayed on her head for a whole month. Every time we attempted to take it off or tried to persuade her to take it off, she would have a fit or cry.

We soon realized that it was her emotional band-aid. You see, up to that point she was the youngest. She was this little blonde that smiled all the time. We used to call her Smiley Riley.

Then Finn was born. All the attention was on him. Oh, do not get me wrong - she loved Finn and was excited to have a baby brother. However, she felt "wounded" that she no longer was the center of attention that the youngest tended to get.

So, to show her feelings, she protested. She put a band-aid on until she felt she was "healed" enough to take it off, which was a month.

Now, this cute little blonde has turned into a beautiful, smart, and talented young lady. She graduates this Saturday and will begin a new adventure in college. I now need to determine if I am going to put on that band-aid or rip it off. All I know is I will be sending Riley off with a box of band-aids in case she needs them. I know I will be keeping a box for myself.

Any fond memories of your kids?

Aunt Renee

One of the fondest memories I have of the family is when my aunts, uncles, and dad got together when I was an adult. You could not help having a smile on your face because of all their antics.

"You can't pick your family; however, you can either laugh with them or at them. Either way, they are still your family. Laughing with them may be safer." anonymous

"You go get it."

"No, I'm not going in there!" Pepe and Perrier are in there!"

My sisters and I hung out by the doorway that led to the basement/family den of Aunt Renee's home.

We were tasked to go down to get something. We had to get past Aunt Renee's guardians, two vicious, protective toy poodles! After rock, paper, scissors I lost. I quietly crept down the stairs. There they were, sleeping on the couch.

I just had to get to the cabinet across from them. I crept silently to the cabinet, opened it, grabbed whatever we needed so desperately, turned. They were up and watching me.

"Pepe and Perrier, good doggies," I said in my sweetest voice. They replied with growls.
I slowly moved back towards the stairs, not taking my eyes off them. Then bolted for the stairs, leaping three steps at a time. I could hear their little nailed paws close behind, their sharp high-pitched yelping echoing behind me. My sisters were at the top encouraging me. "They're right behind you!"

I leaped through the door and my sisters slammed it shut. We could hear scratching at the door.

Now, that is an exaggerated version of Pepe and Perrier (kind-of). They were Aunt Renee's beloved toy poodles, and they were very protective of her. However, like Aunt Renee, their bark was bigger than their bite. Aunt Renee had this deep husky, smoky voice that sounded more like a man's voice. We were afraid of her when we were younger because of that.

However, as we got older, we experienced her true personality. A caring, funny, and loving woman. She was quite a prankster. Something that my dad and she had ongoing wars with.

One of the last times I saw my aunt before her passing was in San Diego, California where several of my uncles and aunts migrated from Massachusetts. It was the summer of 2015. I decided to take a trip out there (that is another story to be told).

My cousins picked me up from the airport and took me directly to the hospital that Aunt Renee was in. Several days before she had fallen out of her bed and broken a hip.

I walked into her room. "Aunt Renee, what are you doing, let's go! I came all the way from Vermont to see you." She smiled and I hugged her.
Later that week Aunt Renee got moved to a rehabilitation facility, which she hated. It was nice and she had a sliding door to a courtyard. I could tell she was unhappy there.

So, I went to her, leaned in, and said, "Just unlock that sliding door and I will break you out later." Which the nearby nurse overheard. I think she checked that door before I left.

I'm sure my dad and his sister, our beloved Aunt Renee, are up in heaven continuing the prank wars along with two little white guardian poodles.

Do you have a memorable aunt?

Uncle Billy

Every family has THAT relative that is the talk of the family. My family has Uncle Billy. I must admit he is my favorite uncle. So, here is a story of Uncle Billy.

Why don't uncles ever get lost? Because they always follow their nephew's GPS "Goofy Positioning System." anonymous.

I sat in Uncle Billie's cluttered back shop of his garage. He sat in his beat-up but comfortable chair on his bench. Various parts lay around and he picked up and fiddled with it as we talked. I sat on a turned over bucket a few feet from him. His guard dog, a beautiful Black German Shepard rested next to me. I would pat her head occasionally to her delight. She was an ex-police dog from Germany, and she only knew German command. I made sure Uncle Billy introduced me before I met her. After the first meeting we were buddies.

Uncle Billy looked like a duck dynasty character. He was in his late 60's, had a long grey beard, receding long grey hair tied back in a ponytail. He was a little overweight but not too bad.
Uncle Billy was married 6 times. He had a way with the ladies. They seem to flock to him. I asked him one day what his secret was. He just shrugged and said, "because I'm a nice guy."

He is now a signal guy. He divorced his 6th wife. Since that divorce there have been numerous girlfriends. An ex-teacher from Alabama, A motorcycle chick who he quickly broke up with because she accidently stabbed her friend because she was trying to stab a dog. (that is a story in itself).

The latest story I heard was the Chinese woman who was 30 years younger than him.
She didn't speak English. I asked him "how did you communicate" he said on my phone. Google translation. She wanted to marry him. He broke that off shortly before he went into the hospital with pancreatitis, which almost killed him. He was ready to meet his maker.
However, his maker wasn't ready for him. Uncle Billy had a 56 Chevy to restore.

Who is your crazy relative?

The Dynamic Duo

I cherish the time I spend with each of my kids, creating memories that last a lifetime.

"The guys who fear becoming fathers don't understand that fathering is not something perfect men do, but something that perfects the man. The end product of child raising is not the child, but the parent." – Frank

Pittman DAD joke: Why did the scarecrow win an award? Because he was outstanding in his field!

The Dynamic Duo leaped down the mountainside trail.

"I'm Batman!" I declared in my deepest, most dramatic voice.

"I'm Robin!" my four-year old son echoed, trying to match my tone with all the strength his little voice could muster.

We bounded down the path, capes (imaginary, of course) billowing behind us. Hikers on their way up stepped aside, grinning as two superheroes charged past them completely immersed in their mission.

My son's fascination with Batman started early. He loved the character so much that he insisted on wearing his Batman costume to church. No one batted an eye. It was just another normal day.

Then there was the time he combined Batman and Superman—wearing a Superman shirt with a Batman mask. That day, he became *SuperBat!*

The *Dynamic Duo* soon became a father-and-son Cub Scout team. Every year, the scouts took a special trip to the Boston Museum, where over a hundred kids and parents spent the night sleeping on the museum floor. We always claimed a spot near the ancient sailing ship exhibits-our own little corner of history and adventure.

Then my son became a teenager, and the *Dynamic Duo* faded into the past. He was more interested in hanging out with his friends than leaping down mountain trails with his dad. But we still found moments together-shooting hoops in the driveway, playing games here and there.

One day, we created a card game called Jace! It started as a game he had learned at camp, though he couldn't quite remember the name or all the rules. So, we made them up as we went. Over time, Jace evolved, with tweaks and refinements, until I finally wrote down the official rules.

One summer day, we sat on the front porch and played Jace from morning until evening. We started when the sun was still casting long shadows by the driveway, and we ended when the golden light stretched across the porch. The only breaks we took were for food and bathroom trips.

Now, my son is taller than me. His voice is deeper. I don't see him as much-he spends a lot of time in his room, chatting with friends and playing games online, a habit formed during the long days of COVID.

But every once in a while, we still break out the cards and play a round or two of Jace. We don't play until sunset anymore-just for an hour, maybe less.

Still, those moments mean everything.

When I feel down, I revisit these little memories, like old movies in my mind and I smile.

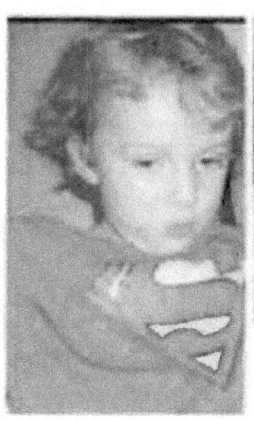  

How did you and your son bond?

The dog chase

I grew up with pets. I believe that a family should have some sort of pet. Sometimes pets can be a pain in the neck. However, you still love them and think of them as part of the family.

"Dogs have boundless enthusiasm but no sense of Shame. I should have a dog as a life coach"-Moby

I was so mad and frustrated. "Sam, get back here!" I shouted.

The golden labradoodle ran to the end of the backyard. "Sam! Bad Dog! You get back here!" I shouted again as I ran after him. Sam thought of this as a game and darted past me heading down our long driveway. I was determined to get this delinquent teen dog. He wasn't going to get away this time! I raced down the driveway yards behind him and gaining. He turned left, leaped over the low fence into the neighbor's yard. I was right behind him. We both sped through the neighbor's yard leaped from another fence into another neighbor's yard. I do not know if any of them were home. I probably would not have noticed anyway because I was intent on getting Sam. My exercise routine was being tested this day. I also think pure adrenaline was kicking in as well.

We raced out of the neighbor's yard and down the sidewalk of the neighborhood. The mailman walking his route leaped out of the way laughing. "Get'em!" he shouted. As I ran past him. I knew Sam thought of this as playing. I did not! He was heading back towards our property. My sides were burning. Sam was hitting his second wind. I dug down and pushed ahead. I finally caught up to him just as he ran for our yard. My daughter came out and he ran right up to her.

"Good Boy!" She said to him.

"No, he isn't!" I said bent over and gasping for air.

Has this ever happened to you?

Nite Nite bear

I never had a stuff animal when I was a kid. However, my kids did. I think almost every family has that ONE item be it a blanket, pillow or stuff animal that was a beloved object to some family member. Well, this is a story of one that has been in the family for two generations.

"Why are Teddy Bears never Hungry? Because they are always stuffed."

"What do you call a Teddy Bear who's lost fur? Fred-bear."

There was a scream of delight. "I found him! I found him!" My 5-year-old daughter squealed as she hugged the ragged, brown, thread-bare teddy bear.

She and her 3-year-old sister started running around the children's library room. Yelling "Nite Nite Bear!"

The Librarian was about to yell at them when I interceded and said, "They found Nite Nite Bear." She looked at me and with a begrudged look and let them celebrate the return of Nite Nite Bear.

He lived with the other stuff animals in the local library for a month. My daughter was distraught when she lost him. Now, she was back again with her beloved Nite Nite Bear.

This teddy bear had a charming life. He was "she" for a brief time then my daughter decided Nite Nite bear was "he". This bear has been in the family for two generations. He was about 30 years old when he became my daughter's bear. He went with her everywhere. He was a part of the family. Even the pets of our family knew not to mess with Nite Nite Bear. Even the dog who tended to tear stuff animals up would not touch Nite Nite Bear.

We went camping at Lake Dunmore one summer. Nite Nite Bear came with us of course.

After the weeklong camping vacation, we headed back home. When we got home. To everyone's horror, Nite Nite Bear didn't come back with us! My daughter was crying. "I left him in the woods" "what if an animal gets him. He will get lonely." I assured her that he is a bear and bears lived in the woods. So, he will be alright. I promised to go search for him first thing in the morning. It was a rough and restless night.

The next morning, I was searching in the woods near where we camped. I felt a little self-conscious because some other family set up camp where we were the previous day. There he was sitting on a rock just where my daughter left him. He was a little damp but ok.

"There you are," I said to him." I hope you had fun with the other bears." I did give him a little hug...This was Nite Nite Bear, after all.

My daughter is now in college. So is Nite Nite Bear. He is now missing his eyes and very thread bare. I offered to fix him up, but my daughter said that he wouldn't be the same.

Did you ever have a beloved stuff animal or object

Guenhwyvar

I have had numerous pets during my lifetime. They all have a special place in my heart. I do not want to say one was better or more favorable than any other. However, I would be lying because there are some that "stand out" over others. Here is the story of Guenhwyvar.

"In ancient times cats were worshiped as gods; they have not forgotten this" Terry Pratchett

"Cats choose us; we don't own them." Kristin Cast

Guenhwyvar (Guinnie) came up from Connecticut with a friend of mine. She was sad to let her go but she had other cats and Guinnie just didn't fit in. She was a sleek short-haired black cat with golden eyes.

I named her after another cat I had when I was a young man. She was a black cat too. However, she was long-haired. The new Guinnie soon became my favorite. I was her human.

She refused to go to the bathroom until her kitty box was set up. She was a little skittish at first when I took her home to the small trailer I lived in at the time. One of the reasons I wanted a cat was that I had a family of mice who scampered around in the wall and the rooms. I was hoping she would be a good mouser. She did deter them from coming out onto the floors. When they did, she played with them but never killed them. We would catch them and relocate them miles from my house.

Several years later we moved to a new house. She now had more room to run and rule. Her kingdom consists of two floors and each room had a wide windowsill. A perfect place to bathe in the sun. She had plenty of places to lounge. She always had her human to lounge on too. Her favorite times to lounge were when I was either having coffee in my recliner or laying on the couch watching a show.

The Day that the "other" furry animal, Bailey, came into the home. Quinnie wasn't too worried. She knew she was The Queen. A couple of times she had to put Bailey in her place. Bailey was not allowed to come near her and her human when they were laying on the couch watching a show. The only time she would "allow" Bailey to be near her human was when they were sitting in the recliner. Quinnie does have a selfless side.

I would find her close to me when I have restless sleep or bad dreams. She was my dream guardian and sleep soother. She even gave her services to my children (Her other humans) when they needed them.

Cat or Dog?

The Flip phone

Your environment can really determine what your personality will grow into. I had the privilege of living both the suburban and country life. As a young adult I had the city life as well. However, I will always cherish the country life. It may be because I lived there the longest and that is where my core values were established. This is one aspect of living in the country.

"Our first impressions are generated by our experiences and our environment, which means that we can change our first impressions . . . by changing the experiences that comprise those impressions."- Malcome Gladwell

I grew up in the suburbs as a kid. When I was a teenager, my settings changed dramatically. I went from riding my bike around the neighborhood with the neighborhood gang to walking in the wilderness with my trusty dog, lady. Oh, I got lost. However, I always managed to survive and find my way home. Luckily my dad taught me basic survival skills like moss always grow more on the north side of the tree and follow the stream downstream and you will eventually find people.

When I turned fourteen, I took a hunter's safety course to further my outdoor education and to hunt with my dad. He even got me my own gun, a Winchester lever-action 30/30. He was an avid hunter, and he always got a deer every year, despite not being the best shot. He was very lucky. I would hit the bull's eye more times than he did during shooting practice. However, I never shot a deer or any animal.

When I was older, I decided that hunting wasn't for me. I enjoyed the wilderness. However, I didn't want to shoot anything. I really appreciated everything my dad taught me, and I knew that if I had to provide for my family by hunting that I could do it. I learned that my dad's real reason for hunting wasn't just to provide meat for the family but to get out into the wilderness. He enjoyed his alone time in the woods.

Years later my dad got a flip phone, and he brought it with him while he was hunting. I would get random calls, early in the morning. "Shawn, guess where I am?"

"You're up in a tree in the middle of the woods."

"How did you know? You're the only one that calls me this early in the morning during hunting season."

He then would describe how beautiful it was where he was and that he had the perfect place for a deer stand. He also commented on how good the reception was when he was high up in the tree stand and mountain.

I now have my own home in the country. I feel blessed that I could enjoy a home in this setting. I passed on some of the wilderness lore to my kids. All my kids furthered their wilderness skills when they went to summer camp. I feel confident that they all could survive in the wilderness if they had to. I also feel that those lessons learned will also help them when they leave the nest and adventure into the world.

Do you have any wilderness tales?

Elderly Care

I had always been brought up to respect my elders. I didn't understand this doctrine fully until I worked at an elderly care place when I was an adult. After experiencing this wonderful, full of life despite their bodies failing, people. Their wisdom, stories, caring nature, and their desire to share their legacies helped me understand the true meaning of "respect my elders."

"We can live our best lives by living a life of gratitude, being thankful for the lessons we've learned through life, and for the people caring for us." anonymous

"Very little is needed to make a happy life; it is all within yourself, in your way of thinking." Marcus Aurelius

I sat under an arbor on a bench in a small, enclosed garden. The air was warm and sunny.

The garden had a wild but organized arrangement of various flowers and plants. A couple of trees provided some shade. Jane sat next to me. She smiled enjoying the sun, flowers, butterflies, and birds.

We both enjoyed each other's company in silence.

I finally broke the silence. "Jane, I need to get inside, now" "I have an activity to get to." She looked a little upset. "Oh, you can stay out longer if you like.

She smiled, mumbled an incoherent sentence, and patted me on the arm. I smiled at her, said goodbye and left her blissfully sitting under the arbor. Jane practically lived outdoors all summer long at her elderly care home.

I worked there every other weekend. My job was basically to entertain the old folks. I couldn't sing or play an instrument, except the programmed electric piano where I performed an enthusiastic version of Bach or Beethoven. I even played "Danny Boy."

However, I could tell stories, read poetry, and talk and listen to the old folks. I even danced occasionally (something only they could appreciate). I once did a quick set of impromptu Irish jigs for St. Patrick's Day, wearing a green leprechaun's hat.

I sometimes sat quietly with them holding their hands. My goal by the end of the shift was to make at least one elderly person smile. I achieved this every time.

I never thought I would ever work at a place like this. The reason I was there was that I needed another job. I started as a concierge. I moved into another position because of staff changes. I asked the director of the activities if they needed help. Chatting with the old folks that came up to the desk was something I enjoyed. My respect and love for the elderly were reinforced because of this job change. We will all be there one of these days. My hope for everyone is that you will not be alone and that someone will be there for you in your last days.

Do you ever think of what you will like when you are older?

George and Peg

I've been working with the elderly for a few years now. There are so many stories that these lovely human beings share. Here is but one story from an older couple.

"Do not grow old, no matter how long you live. Never cease to stand like curious children before the great mystery into which we were born." Albert Einstein

I sat with George and Peg. George was deep in concentration, humming to himself as he looked for pieces of a puzzle. Peg, his wife, was there being supportive and to be close to her beloved husband of over many years. I sat with both, helping George with the puzzle. I don't like puzzles. However, this was more for George than for me.

I admired George's and Peg's relationship. They were high school sweethearts. She was a teacher, and he was a pilot in the air force. He flew bombers during the Korean War. They raised six kids and lived a successful life. They now live in this elderly care facility that I worked at part-time. George lovingly pushed Peg around the facilities and made sure she was involved with many activities, even if she fell asleep during it.

I remember the day that Peg passed. I respectfully kept my distance from the large family that came in to say goodbye to their mom, grandma, Great Grandma, and aunt. I talked to family members occasionally when it was appropriate. I indicated how wonderful she was and let them tell me stories about her. I got to learn who Peg was from multiply points of view.

A few weeks later everything was a little calmer. I sat patiently with George in his apartment as he showed me his air force medals and pictures. Something that I have heard and seen numerous times before. He then started to talk about Peg. He told me things I had never heard about her. I just sat there and listened. I didn't say a word and nodded or smiled at the appropriate times. I could sense more than hear that this was something that he needed to do. I felt honored and privileged that George felt comfortable enough with me to talk and show his feelings.

Do you know of any high school sweethearts?

Childhood and Young Adult

"In childhood be modest, In youth temperate, In Adulthood just and in old age prudent" Socrates.

The Little Red House on Glenn Street

This next short story is dedicated to my mom who passed away this past Wednesday May 13th, 2020.

I know some of you will be sad reading this, however I hope it will put a smile on your face as well. At the corner of Glenn Street and Jasper Street there was a little red house.

"When you finally go back to your old home, you find it wasn't the old home you missed but your childhood."
- Sam Ewing

A pine tree with a low brick wall behind it was in the front yard. A huge yellow flowered bush was off to the right front yard near the road. It was so big that we used it as a fort.

We had an apple tree on the right side of the yard near the neighbor's border. You could see the whole neighborhood if you climbed to the top of this tree.

In the summertime cars lights would shine in the side yard as they came down the road. The drivers would see frozen kids standing in the yard. A popular game we played was "freeze car".

The red house had a porch in front of a one-story kitchen. The rest of the house to the left of the porch and kitchen was two stories. In the two-story section was the living room divided by an L shape half wall, which created two living rooms. A small bedroom was off the living room. I remember mom trying to show me the waltz in the bigger living room.

All the kids' rooms could be reached by the narrow stairway, located on the left side of the living room next to the wall. The 1st room as you reached the top was my older sister's room. Next to that was my room and the last room was the younger sister's room. You had to walk through all the rooms to get to each room.

My room's window opened out onto the roof of the kitchen. We older kids would climb out on it and walk over to the brick chimney that was on the far side of the roof. We did this of course when mom wasn't looking or paying attention.

When us kids "drove our mom up the wall" or "drove a saint to drink!", two popular sayings that my mom used when we frustrated her. She would say "go to your rooms!" and if we didn't comply quickly enough, she would chase us with the broom up the stairs. She would stand at the bottom waving her broom, while watching us kids scramble pulling each other away from the top of the stairs so we were not the last one up the stairs. Mom never hit us but I'm sure there was a smile on her face as we frantically got up the stairs.

I remember mom showing us a magic trick while sitting at the kitchen table. She had this trick of plucking money from inside our ears. The kitchen was also the place where us kids had to kneel in the corner underneath the phone if we were bad. My younger sister Cathi spends many hours there.

The kitchen also had a fireplace there. Mom would help us pop popcorn using an old fashion long handled popper. The fireplace was also where we would have the occasional bat that would create havoc In the O'Neil household. A person passing by would see kids running franticly around with hands over their heads and the mom yelling "Get it! get it!" at the top of her lungs while imitating the kids. The father would be chasing with a fishing net. Sometimes when my dad wasn't there. I would have to be the one to "get it"!

Mom also made our favorite quick cheap meal in that kitchen. English muffins baked with tuna fish, a tomato and melted cheese. I cannot remember the name we gave it, but it is like tuna melt.

That little red house is no longer a little red house. It is still there but has changed color, structure and the yard are completely different. You probably could not recognize it as once a little red house. However, the little red house on Glen Street will always be in my memories and I will see my mom chasing us kids up the stairs, running frantically covering her head and dancing with me in the living room. Mom, I hope there is a little red house for you in the afterlife

Do you remember your childhood home?

The Dark Road

Friends and memories! When I think back on the stupid, dangerous things that my friends and I did, I am surprised that I am still alive. Here is a less "dangerous" but stupid event that I had with my childhood friends who I still stay in contact to this day.

"Friendship is the hardest thing in the world to explain. It's not something you learn in school. But if you haven't learned the meaning of friendship, you really haven't learned anything." - Muhammad Ali

"The most beautiful discovery true friends make is that they can grow separately without growing apart." Elisabeth Foley.

One night when I was in my teens. I was sitting in my room when two of my friends burst into my room. "Shawn, what are you doing right *now*?" "Do you want to go for a ride somewhere?"

"Ummm! Sure!" I was just doing homework, after all. We jumped into Dave's little Volkswagen Rabbit and drove off.

I lived in the backwoods of a small Vermont town. All dirt roads lead even further into the backwoods. "Where does this road go."

"Oh, that's a dead end." "Let's check it out."

The dirt road had a big hill, came to a fork which I knew both led to dead ends.

"Oh, I guess you were right." Dave turned around. As he was turning around, he "accidentally" dropped his hat out the window. "Oh, I dropped my hat" "Shawn, can you get that for me." "Ok". I said wondering why he dropped his hat out the window.

I got out to pick it up and they took off. "That was mean," I said out loud.

It was a dark night, and I was in the middle of nowhere. I started walking down the dark dirt road. I felt like I was being watched. I kept looking back but could not see anything.

So, I moved a little faster. I heard a rock "fall" onto the road. I moved even more quickly. Suddenly, something dark burst out of the woods behind me grunting and howling.

I took off running at full speed down the hill. I caught up to "my friends" who were waiting down the bottom of the hill. I jumped into the car. "Let's go! Let's go! There is something behind me!" I yelled.

"What?" "No, there isn't." They replied doubtfully. "Let's go look". We decided to walk up to look. Now, everything we did was what you "don't" do if you saw any horror movie.

We started walking up. In the dark. That is when it dawned on me. "This is a trick!"

We walked up to the turnaround part. I picked up a rock when they were not looking and threw it in the woods. "What was that?!" "Ok, Michael! You can come out now."

No reply. We ran down to the car, jumped in, and drove back to my house. There was Michael in the house eating pizza that my parents ordered.

"Hi, guys!" Where were you? "I hope there is pizza left for us!" we said glaring at him.

Have you participated in any pranks?

Rainy day

Rain pellets strike the windowpane. A rhythmic beat of thousands of tiny drums. The musical number that lulls you back to sleep. Snuggled into your favorite comfy blanket or getting a little closer to that loved one be it a human or furry kind.

Rain is such a cleansing element. It washes away the dirt both symbolic and literal. People may complain that it is raining "there goes my day." However, if they look at it as a living substance, not a deterrent. Yes, there is always "Too much" but that is with everything if you think about it. Your attitude may become more positive.

"Life is not about waiting for the storm to pass. It's about learning to dance in the rain." – Vivian Greene

"Rain is nature's way of washing the world clean." - William Shakespeare

"I never saw a rain cloud I didn't want to dance with." - Dolly Parton

A memory that has stayed with me to this day of a rain situation that happened at a campground.

The orchestra of rain played overture on our tents. The day started sunny and full of running around the campgrounds, swinging on the camp swings. There were other families with their tents pitched in their designated areas. We had one close to the camp road.

It was like a battlefield when the rain started. People ran for cover, trying to dodge the barrage of raindrops. People duck into their tents. Some are leaping for any cover. It was amazing how quickly people disappeared into their safe shelters of tents. Then there was a calm, and the campground was empty. Voices could be heard coming from the various campsites. Families huddled together. Kids talking excitedly from the sudden change in weather.

Suddenly the empty, quiet wet campgrounds were interrupted by a commotion. My dad exploded out of our tent carrying my stepmom. She was screaming and laughing at the same time. "Put me down, Dick, put me down!" He made it a few feet and promptly lost his footing, and they crashed down together in a puddle getting even more soaked. They both were laughing and splashing like the kids that soon joined them into the wet arena. Other families peered out from the safety of their tents to see this family romping through the playground, laughing, splashing, chasing, rolling, sliding. Soon the merriment of my family became contagious. Other families began to emerge from their dry shelters to partake in the fun splash fest. Who said rain spoiled any fun?

Fun in the Rain?

Moving Out

Growing up in a large family can be fun and challenging. Especially when it came to sharing a bedroom with a sibling.

My favorite room in my house is my bedroom; my private space where I can go to do my reading or listen to music. Shirley Ballas

We grew up in a small house with four bedrooms. I shared a bedroom with my three brothers. But I enjoy the way that I was brought up. It kept me hungry. It kept me humble. Scottie Pippen

The car was packed, and my parents and I were heading out to travel to my college. My little sister and brother were watching from the living room window. As soon as the car was driving out of the driveway they sprang into action. They rushed to the bedroom downstairs and moved my sister's stuff out of the room they shared for many years up to my now vacant room.

I was the first out of the house and they were taking advantage of the "extra room". The sister who would be the next one out of the house looked at them incredulity. "He hasn't even left the driveway, and you are taking over his room!" She yelled at them. They didn't pay attention because of how focused they were on this separation of siblings.

Like most big families that only lived in houses that had fewer bedrooms than kids, siblings had to bunk up together. It usually was the younger ones or the same-sex ones. In our household growing up, it was the former that bunked up. Bedrooms tended to be occupied by whoever was left. While we were residents in our bedrooms, we were allowed to make it over or make it our own. The middle sister made great efforts to make sure her room was unique. So, she painted it black with red polka dots.

My room was more spartan. It was just a place for me to sleep and daydream in. However, I did put some posters up on the walls to add a little character. So, when I left my sister had an open canvas to make the room her own.

Like my childhood home, I have a similar situation, not enough bedrooms, and too many kids. However, I moved into the house while the oldest was in college. So, the two remaining kids got their bedrooms. The difficulty came when they were all home at the same time. The two girls were "done" being roommates since they were most of their lives. We had to come up with creative sleeping alternatives like putting up portable partitions in bedrooms or making the living room a comfortable sleeping place. All I know is that I am enjoying the inconvenience because I know that someday, I will be an empty nester and will miss my kids.

Do you remember when you left home?

Morning Run

In my youth I had a much better drive and discipline to stay healthy. Something I want to bring back to my old age.

"Two roads diverged in a wood, and I took the one less traveled by, and that has made all the difference." Robert Frost

I crawled out of bed. The beeping of my alarm is still ringing in my head. I hit snooze for the third time. I finally hit "off" while sitting on my bed. My shorts, t-shirt, and running shoes are sitting on the bureau next to my bed. Calling me, reminding me of the commitment I set for myself. I groggily pull on my running clothes, stumble downstairs to my family home.

Dad sits in his chair drinking coffee.

"Good morning, Sunshine!" he says in an exaggerated, annoying, cheerful voice.

He is wearing his appliance uniform with the name "Dick" embroidered on the front pocket. He has been up since the crack of dawn.

I grunt and smile weakly. "Morning" I mumble as I amble past him like the living dead. "Have a good run!" he says still in that exaggerated, annoying cheerful voice.

I wave weakly at him as I leave the living room.

The morning is crisp for a summer day. I am finally waking up after running for a little bit.
The world is quiet as I run down the tree-lined dirt road.

I see a dark brown form up ahead on a branch above the road. A great horned owl peers down at me from the branch. "Morning," I say to it as I run underneath it. The Owl turns its head and looks at me. Shortly afterward, it flies past me and lands on a branch down the road in front of me.

My escort follows me down the forested, dirt road for a few minutes then decides to be done and sits on the last branch and watches me disappear down the road. When I returned it was gone.

I felt blessed and honored to have that experience. It was an event that happened only once during my daily morning runs down the forested dirt road. Perhaps this was an omen that I was running down the right path.

Do you have a morning routine?

Halloween

October is here! Which means kids will be taken to the streets dressed in costumes asking for Candy, Halloween!

"Halloween was confusing. All my life my parents said, 'Never take candy from strangers.' And then they dressed me up and said, 'Go beg for it.' " Rita Rudner

"Have you come to sing pumpkin carols?" Linus (It's the Great Pumpkin, Charlie Brown)

"There is a child in every one of us who is still a trick-or-treater looking for a brightly lit front porch." Robert Brault

It was Halloween. I wore a cheap plastic mask and thin material over my thick winter jacket. I was a puffy overweight superhero. Probably Batman or Spiderman. I don't even remember what my sisters wore, except we all had puffy winter jackets incorporated in our costumes. We lived in a suburban neighborhood where it came alive with the dead, creepy, and insane facade. An intense competition of elaborate displays was rampant throughout the neighborhood.

My dad and mom didn't get into the competition with our house. However, my dad did get into the spirit of Halloween in the form of a tiger. (His nickname from his football days) We were escorted around the neighborhood by this almost 6-foot-tall walking tiger. The tiger would disappear sometimes and leap out with a roar scaring unexpected witches, vampires, ghouls, and superheroes, as well as the escorting parents. Oh, and if you were a troop of unruly, unsupervised teenagers. You will lose your candy if you drop it while running away from this wild beast. Well, so I was told by the tiger. I never saw it happen, but he did have some extra candy when we got home.

Forty years later, this Halloween scene repeats itself in a different state in a smaller suburb neighborhood. My children, similarly, costumed with their cheap plastic mask puffy jackets, ran from doorstep to doorstep with plastic pumpkin pail banging on their sides. The intense Halloween displays competitions were still rampant with slightly better technology.

A tiger was roaming the neighborhood at one point, and it may or may not have returned to my home with extra candy.

What was your best and worst Halloween costume?

The swimming quarry

Ah summertime! Longer days, hotter weather, green as far as the eye can see (if you are in Vermont) and swimming holes! These are a few things when I think of summer.

What do you call seagulls that live near the bay? Bagels.

What do you call it when a guy throws his laptop into the ocean? Adele, Rollin' in the Deep.

The red Volkswagen bus was crowded with a bunch of young people heading for the Williston swimming quarry. Jim, the owner, cruised along the road at the top speed of 45 miles per hour. If the bus went faster than that it would shudder and shake.

The quarry was located near St Michael's College; farmlands surrounded it at that time. People would park on the side of the road avoiding the electric fence that kept the cows in.
It was a hot summer that year and the quarry was occupied throughout the days, especially during the weekends. Many years ago, the quarry had flooded, and it became the locals' place to swim. There was a rope tied to a tree that people used to swing out and drop 20 or 30 feet into the deep waters. It was rumored that there was an old steam shovel on the bottom of the deep quarry.

We all piled out of the bus, avoiding the electric fence, and headed down the forested path that led to the quarry. People were there already. People were swinging from the rope or diving off the quarry wall. There was a footpath that led up to the top from the water.

After a long day of playing in the quarry we all started back to the red bus. I was the first one there. While I was opening the passenger side door I bent over to move away from the door. I didn't realize how close I was to the electric fence. I bent slightly and my posterior touched the electric fence. Now, remember I just came back from swimming, so I was wet. A jolt went through my body. Not really thinking but reacting I grabbed the nearest thing, which happened to be the metal antennae of the red bus. I was fully grounded, wet, and touched by a great conductor. So, I did the only thing I could do, break the connection. I ripped the antenna off the bus out of pure desperation.

Moments later I was sweating and leaning against the bus. Everyone came back and wondered what happened. I'm not sure if anyone saw what happened, I was a little too occupied to care. However, I did notice that there was a red weld mark against both my cheeks.
Lesson learned: Don't Park next to electric fences when you go swimming.

Do you have a favorite place to hang out with your friends?

The Projectionist

I've worked many different jobs throughout my life. One of the more memorable ones was working as a film projectionist at a college. I saw many different movies from artsy films to blockbusters. Here is one of those memorable times.

At a job interview. "Can you perform under pressure?" No, but I can try Bohemian Rhapsody!

The theater was crowded, and the movie was about to begin. The lights just would not go off. I and the student worker turned the switches off, all the light switches. Nothing! The movie just starting with the beginning credits. Suddenly a white-haired elderly man walked into the "employees only" booth and started hitting switches (the ones we had already tried). "Sir, this is an employee's only space. Can you please leave," I said politely but sternly.

"You need to get these lights off!" he demanded. "Yes, sir, we are aware of it, and we are working on it. Please leave." He mumbled something incoherent and walked out of the booth.

I finally went to the breaker box and turned off any breaker that said lights. It worked just as the beginning credits were ending.

Later I found out that the white-haired gentleman that had walked into the booth was the Film Department Chair. We got to know each other throughout the years after that.

The projectors in the booth were older 35mm/16mm film projectors. There were two. One had to switch to the other projector when you were showing long films. A projectionist was trained to splice the film together (physically tape films to each other), thread the film onto the projectors, watch for the dots in the movie so they would know when to switch over to the other projector, and to fix the film if it broke.

The last thing was important to know, especially on one occasion. A student worker and I were showing an important film which the producer was there to talk about. He brought the film to us, and we spliced it together. Unfortunately, part of the film was brittle (which does happen). Towards the beginning of the film, it broke. We quickly took it down and started to repair it. This was the students' first time showing a film. She had plenty of training and I picked her because of her aptitude and maturity in handling situations. She went to work on the film while I went out to appease the crowd.

"Sorry, there was technical difficulty, and the film will start momentarily." I quickly went back into the booth and helped her finish the repair and put the film back up on the projector. We were both fast and efficient. The film was only down for a few minutes.

After sighing with relief, my worker asked me if she could keep the one broken frame we fixed. I said it was ok. We would have thrown it away anyway. She wanted a memento from her first film.

Years later she came back to visit after she graduated. She came up to me and showed me the film frame. She had carried it in her wallet since that memorable day.

What was the most odd or memorable job you had?

The Mine

When I think back on my youthful adventures, I sigh with relief that I am still alive. Here is one of those adventures.

"You will do foolish things but do them with enthusiasm."- Colette

"Reckless youth makes rueful age." - Benjamin Franklin

We were hiking in the mountains of Aspen, Colorado. We learned from locals that there were abandoned mines up in the mountains. We were determined to find one and explore it. We were young, adventurous, foolish young men. We set out with backpacks with the things we thought we might need for exploring water, flashlights, trail mix, I may have had a Swiss Army Knife. I do not recall what else. We would find later that the flashlights were very important.

We hiked to a spot on the path, which a local old-timer described to us, then got off it. We hiked deep into the mountains. The entrance was easy to find when you got close to it. It was a dark hole in the side of a hill. We had to bend down to enter but once we were in, we could stand up. Because of how the entrance was dug the mine became dark quickly even on a bright summer day. We turned our flashlights on. Our goal was to find the center of the mine. We were told that miners dug tunnels until they got deep enough into the mountain, then they would widen it into a central mine.

We found the tunnel that we thought would lead to the central mine. We started in a low crouch, then soon ended up crawling through tunnels. My friend was ahead of me. We came upon tight spots where the tunnel had caved in a little. Foolishly, we pressed on. We would come upon old thick wooden support beams occasionally. After crawling for a while, we decided to see how dark it was in the tunnels, so we both stopped and turned our flashlights off. The void was so dark and quiet. If it weren't for our breathing it would seem we did not exist. That we were just thoughts in an empty void. After a while, we gladly turned our lights back on.

After crawling for what seemed like an eternity we came to the central mine. There were old train tracks with an old metal cart. We felt a breeze, so we knew there was at least another exit somewhere and air. The central mine was perhaps 20 feet by 30 feet. We ate lunch, then looked around for another exit. The breeze must have been from air holes, or the other exits were caved in. There were small beams of light that came down from a scattering of small holes that opened to the sunny day above us. Nothing big enough to crawl through.

We were relieved to get back to the sunny Colorado day. Years later when I think back to that foolish and dangerous day, I realize that we could have died if any of those tunnels fully caved in. We would have been trapped. However, I am here now to tell this tale.

What is the most dangerous thing you did?

I had my Lady as a boy

Every family has a favorite pet, be it a dog, cat, bird, or lizard. I have had several pets throughout my life. However, the pet that is dearest to my heart (sorry Bailey) is My Lady.

What do you get when you cross a dog and a calculator? A friend you can count on.
Cats are smarter than dogs. You can't get eight cats to pull a sled through snow.

I had my Lady as a boy. She was gorgeous. She had one blue eye and one brown eye. She had long soft brown hair. Lady was the runt of a litter of a dozen pups. Generally, runts were harassed. She was not accepted at first. She was the smartest pup. Lady learned that if she got to the bowl of food and sat in it, the other pups could not shove her away. She ate at her leisure.

When she was older and about the size of a fox, which she resembled, we would take long walks in the extensive woods of Vermont. A wilderness area that had all kinds of wild animals. Lady was my trusting, loyal and protective friend, always at my side. She would sleep with me on my bed. Be there to greet me in the morning. We really protected each other during those long walks in the woods. We met various animals from bears to porcupines. We both knew how to be quiet and respectful. Lady only barked if they got too close or threatening, which rarely happened.

We had other pets in the family as well. However, Lady bonded with me and became my faithful companion.

It was a sad day when I left for college. I'm sure she wondered where I was for days. She would have slept on my bed if it was there. Since there were several kids in the family, and I was the first to go off to college, my room was occupied by my younger sister. Lady went to the next best companion, my dad.

My dad took her everywhere with him. He also assured me that she missed me and will always be My Lady.

What pet did you bond with?

Winter Cave

It seems that when you are younger you tend to do "foolish" things regardless of anyone's advice. (Especially your parents.) However, part of growing up is learning from those decisions and hopefully surviving them.

"Never tell a young person that anything cannot be done. God may have been waiting centuries for someone ignorant enough of the impossible to do that very thing." - G. M. Trevelyan

I had three layers of clothes on, and I was wrapped in a sleeping bag. My big furry puppy lay by my feet. I was in a shallow cave in the dead of winter. My stepbrother slept similarly dressed, except with no puppy at his feet, next to me. A part of the cave had a rocked off section that had a hole going up, like a natural chimney. We had a fire going in the nook. We still froze that night. The only thing that was warm on me was my feet because that is where my puppy slept.

I can't imagine what it would have been like if we hadn't had the fire.

My dad thought we were fools for sleeping in a cave in the dead of winter. However, he let us do it, saying we would be back before the morning ended. We could walk the half mile down the mountain and sleep in our cozy warm house. However, we were stubborn teenage boys. Determined to last the night in below zero temperatures in a cave and to prove dad wrong.

The cave was shallow, six- or seven-feet in. We couldn't stand up in it. Two teens and a puppy barely fit in it. I found it in one of my numerous explorations of the mountainous woods behind my house. There were some other caves that might have been better.
However, we didn't want to take the chance of disturbing its resident, who ho we thought might have been a bear based on the scat and prints around the cave.

We made it through the night! As soon as the sun rose in the early morning sky we packed up and headed home. No fingers or toes were lost from frostbite. We shivered a little despite all the layers of clothes on us. We couldn't wait to have a hot meal and stand by the woodstove.
I noticed fresh suspicious boot prints near our cave, as we trekked down the mountain. We lost them when we went into the dense pine forest.

When we got to the house my dad was sitting in his chair drinking a cup of coffee. "There is hot water on the stove for hot cocoa if you want any," he said, as he scuffed the puppy who had just jumped up on his lap. "Dad, did you check on us?" I asked. "Why would I do that? You're the ones who wanted to spend the night in the dead of winter in a cave. Plus, you are here, so you made it." I smirked at him and said, "Yaa, right."

He smiled and continued petting the puppy.

Sometimes when I am in a tough situation, I look for footprints in the snow. Many times, they are there. I then know that I still have someone looking out for me.

Where was the strangest place you stayed?

Trust me

It was a summer day in the backwoods of Starksboro. My dad and I were working on a brush pile. I was up close to the pile throwing little branches and sticks on the pile. Suddenly a huge branch barely missed me. I turned around to see my father grabbing another big branch, ready to throw it onto the pile. "Dad! You almost hit me." He looked at me and said, "Trust me." Trusting my dad, I turned around and continued my job. The next thing I knew I was waking up to my father's face looming over me. "Are you ok?" I just looked at him, got up, walked away, and said, "I trusted you!"

"My father didn't tell me how to live. He lived and let me watch him do it." — Clarence Budington Kelland

That moment was the start of more comical experiences with my dad. Every time we were doing any physical labor together and one of us said "trust me" we would get laughing so hard that one of us would end up getting hurt.

Do not get me wrong. My dad was a great dad, and I trusted him. However, when it came to any physical things that we did together like moving a refrigerator (he was an appliance man) we thought it would be best if other people did it.

I now have a 14-year-old boy and every time we work together on a physical project I think fondly of my dad. I tell the tales of Papa Richie, who my son has never met because my dad passed away before he was born. However, I think my dad looks down from heaven and says to my son, "Trust him."

What memory reminds you of a loved one?

The Duffy

Friendships. Did you ever have one of those friends that you have known forever? You have not seen them in years; however, when you do meet you pick up where you left off. Time doesn't matter.

"If you have friends as weird as you, then you have everything."- Unknown

"Friends come and go, like the waves of the ocean... But the true ones stay, like an octopus on your face. Best friends don't care if your house is clean. They care if you have wine."- Unknown.

I raced down the dirt road on my brand new black Huffy! I sat on a wide comfortable seat. My hands gripped the rubber padded handlebars. I stood up on the pedals feeling the wind rush past me. I was going fast! The wide rubber studded tires absorbed the rocky terrain. I had no helmet or any other protective gear. I was 14 and this was the eighties.

I was headed down to meet my new friend Kevin, who sat behind me in school. His dad was the minister of the village and their house, the parsonage, was right next to the school and across from the church. I had to make the three-mile trek, which was all downhill. No problem for a kid on his Huffy.

When I got there, I met Kevin and his older brother Robbie. There were other local kids hanging out there as well. Everyone was impressed and envious of my Huffy. It was the bike that every kid wanted to own during those days.

There was a ditch just in front of the parsonage garage. Robbie dared me to jump it on my Huffy. It was after all, a Huffy and it could take such a jump. Before anyone could say anything, I rode my bike to the end of the road. The house was on a side road off the main road. I pedaled as fast as I could towards the ditch. Robbie's eyes went wide, and he started to say something. But I was too committed. I hit the edge of the ditch, soared into the air, and hit the other side. Well, my front wheel hit the slightly pitched edge, and the rest of my bike fell into the ditch. My bike now resembles a chopper bike. The front spoke bent from the impact. Robbie came up to me and said, "I was about to tell you that you should jump it the other way."

Later, I was riding my wobbly, bent bike up the hilly dirt road that I soared down earlier. Forty years later my good friends Rob (he is an adult now, so Robbie doesn't fit anymore) and Kevin remind me of that fated day that I jumped my bike into a long, wonderful friendship, We and other friends had many adventures in our small rural Vermont homes.

Who are the friends that you still keep in touch with?

The Cow Field

Everyone has a special place that they went to as kids. A place that may be a private place, or one where all the neighborhood kids went to play and explore.

"I stopped by my childhood home and asked the owners politely whether I could have a look around. They immediately said no and slammed the door in my face. My parents can be so rude sometimes."-Unknown.

"What's your favorite childhood memory?" "Not paying bills."-Unknown

On summer days in the 1970s, my sisters and I were kicked out of the house in the morning and were told not to come back until it got dark. I always wondered If this was standard practice that all parents in the 70s said this to their kids in the summer. Regardless, we gladly were obedient kids.

This was before cell phones, computers and all the other electronic devices that kids have these days. The only way my mother could get ahold of us was to yell out the front door: "Kids, it's time for dinner!" For some reason every kid in the neighborhood knew their parents' distinctive yell. If they missed the call their friends were sure to let them know. "Your mom is yelling for you."

Our local neighborhood hang-out was the "Cow Field," which was a distinctive place because I grew up in a suburban town that had only one farm. This was an enchanted land for us kids. It had a great sledding hill in the winter, a pine forest to play hide and seek in or build forts, and a river that was accessible by a path through the pine forest into the hardwoods area. Oh, and there were cows.

We still have fond memories of this children's paradise. In fact, many years later when I became a parent, I happened to be down where I grew up visiting relatives. So, I was curious if this childhood memory was still there. I drove my kids past the house I grew up in. It had changed quite a bit. It wasn't the little red house I remember. It was a different color and there was an added extension to it.

However, I was happily surprised to see that the cow field was still there! It had not changed one bit. In fact, there were still cows grazing in the upper field before the sledding hill. The next generation got to see this enchanted land that had meant so much to me as a kid.

Where is your favorite childhood place?

Siblings did the most stupid things

Siblings did the most stupid and sometimes cruel things to each other. Most of the time it was the older ones coaxing the younger ones. It is a miracle that we all survived to adulthood despite these stupid events.

"I brought home new backpacks for my kids. and they fought over who got which one. They are identical backpacks." - Valeria

"Brothers and sisters can say things to one another that no one else can." - Gregory E. Lang

"The greatest gift our parents ever gave us was each other." - Unknown

One of the things that my father taught all the kids when we were younger was how to fish.

My sisters and I would fish at various places around our hometown in Massachusetts. One summer day the three oldest siblings were fishing at a local reservoir.

One of the daunting tasks was patience and waiting for the pole to jerk before excitedly reeling the line in, but not too fast so you wouldn't lose the fish. However, the most challenging thing was putting the worm on the hook.

Grabbing a squirming, slimy worm, impaling it several times on a hook so it stayed there, then casting it into the water. My younger sister really didn't like this task, but she put on a brave face and would do it.

One day she was struggling with an overly squirmy worm. She ended up impaling her thumb instead of the worm. She held her thumb out, crying. "Ouch! Help me get it off."

My older sister and I looked at her and I came to the rescue. After several jerks and ouches. I managed to get the hook off her thumb. She did what every kid did when they had a cut thumb, sticking it in her mouth.

My older sister saw this and said "Oh, no!" "What?! What?!" said my younger sister "It may be infected, now."

"No!!! What do I do?"

We happened to have a bottle of vinegar. (Why we had it I have no clue).

My older sister picked it up and said, "In order to not get infected you have to drink this bottle of vinegar" (8 ounces I think).

I added, "yeah, and you have to drink the whole bottle, or it will not work."

Moments later my little sister was heaving on the ground, but she didn't have an infection anymore.

What was the stupidest or meanest thing you did to a sibling?

Poison Ivy

Every family has THAT family car or vehicle. One that was either remembered with fond memories or one that they try to forget. My first car was a Yugo. This was a memory that I tried to forget.

"How do you double the value of a Yugo? Fill it with gas."
"If someone named Patricia owns a station wagon...Does that make it a Patti-wagon?"

It was the 1970s. A bright green van with poison ivy leaves craftily painted on the sides cruised up route 89 heading for Vermont. I sat in the front passenger's seat? with my 4 sisters glaring at me. I did win the draw. It was a four hour drive up to Vermont and I got the first time slot.

My sisters jockeyed for position in between the driver's seat and passenger's seat. Which was really an uncomfortable position because they had to kneel. However, whoever got to that position could see out the windshield. The rest of the kids sat on the benches or lay on the queen-sized bed that was at the end of the van. Yes, this was the 70s. Seats belts were not mandatory.

"Poison Ivy" was my dad's pride and joy. He spent many days customizing it. It had all the luxuries of a camper. Cabinets, cupboards, even a sink. He didn't have a stove, but he did have a propane campers' stove that he could hook up either on the small counter in the van or outside the van. He even made a fiberglass canoe painted green with little poison Ivy painted on the side, which he called "Little Ivy". We would strap it to the top of the van to have on our camping adventure.

We kids would be waiting at our mom's house, listening to the roar of Poison Ivy to pick us up to bring us to our Vermont summer adventures.

Favorite vehicle?

New Year's Tradition

The New Year may be just a point in time. However, it seems we all have some sort of tradition to celebrate the changing of the year. Here are some of my traditions.

"What is a New Year's resolution? Something that goes out one year and out the other" -Unknown

I raced in my car to my hometown. Yes, I was going over the speed limit. However, I had a short time before the New Year began. It was a tradition in my older teenage years to celebrate the turning of the new year at my "second" family's house, which was the parsonage of my hometown. I was coming back from Burlington, where I had been celebrating the other tradition, watching a movie with my friend Rob just before the New Year. We always managed to get back to Rob's home to toast the New Year.

Unfortunately, my car had issues and began to sputter and slow down just as I was heading up the hill in my town. I was perhaps 5 miles away and the clock was ticking. Rob was driving his car way ahead of me. This was before cell phones so there was no way to contact anyone. I just prayed that my car would make it to the house on time. Going at a snail's pace, I sputtered into the house, just let the car die in their parking spot next to the house, leaped out and ran into the house. The ball to New York Times Square was dropping on the TV as I ran in. I made it!

My traditions changed through the different New Years. When I was a young man living in Burlington, I tended to go to New Year parties. Sometimes toasting the new year with friends and strangers, at a local establishment. Sometimes at a friend's house. The one tradition that I observed when I was a young man and beyond was to never get drunk on New Year. I wanted to be in my own senses to experience the start of a new year. Forget resolutions. I never kept them no matter how dedicated I was to them. I think the longest I lasted was perhaps a month.

Once I became a dad my New Year tradition changed. I now have a family and kids to celebrate the New Year. It was a privilege for them when they were younger to be able to stay up until midnight. Most of the time they made it. We would toast with sparkling cider.

This new year was especially memorable. Because it was over! I knew that the new reality that the pandemic brought to the world would forever change how we looked at our lives. The virus couldn't care less about our human concept of time. However, this concept of time could be thought of as a gauge or milestone for the hope that we can conquer this. I will put some effort into thinking this way. One thing that history has taught us is that we humans are resilient.

Do you have a New Year's tradition?

Falling and Flying

Hopefully this story will bring this one to new heights.

"How do you open a parachute?" "I need answers quickly please."

"I had my first parachute jump today and was so terrified! This guy strapped himself to me, we jumped out of the plane and as we plummeted, he said..." "So, how long have you been an instructor?"

I sat at the edge of a 1000- or 2000-foot drop. Air flew past me, and the sounds of the small airplane were all around me. "You're next! Ready?" The skydiving instructor shouted at me as he tapped me' on the shoulder. I smiled weakly at him and stood up. He attached the static line to the support. I climbed out onto the strut that supported the wings. I haven't looked down on it yet. I hung from the wing and looked at the instructor. "Don't let go until you smile." He yelled at me over the noise. I gave a weak smile, then flung backwards off the wing. All fear and anxiety left me. I figured It didn't matter now; I was already 100% committed. The static line pulled my parachute. I looked up and checked my lines to make sure everything was ok. At this point it was purely instinctual. The intense training was showing its worth as I prepared to jump a couple of thousand feet over a prison in Malone, New York.

I looked down; Jim was a couple of hundred feet below me. He was the first to jump. I followed him down. "Whoo Hoooo, I'm flying!" I yelled into the open sky.

A bird was below me and I gave chase. I pulled one of my toggles and started to spiral, something the instructor insisted that we try. I was flying! Although the ground was approaching me slowly. My adrenaline must have been spiking at this point. I felt alive. There was a huge painted bullseye way below me. We were supposed to land as close to that as possible. I forgot about those instructions because I was flying! Jim landed a few feet away from the bullseye. I aimed at it as close as I could to it. When I got a few feet from the ground I pulled both toggles, which created an air cushion between me and the ground. I slowly glided to the ground. My training kicked in and I rolled like I was taught. However, I really didn't have to because I touched down so lightly that I could have walked away easily. Life can be like this sometimes. The fear of falling can be overwhelming. However, sometimes you need to look up and see that you have a parachute above you. Then you can enjoy life and fly!

Have you done anything adventurous?

Traveling and Strangers

"May the road rise up to meet you. May the wind be always at your back. May the sunshine warm upon your face; the rains fall soft upon your fields and until we meet again, may God hold you in the palm of His hand."

Irish blessing

The Wishing Well

I just returned from a wonderful trip from Ireland. I have many short stories of my adventures there. I decided to share them in these next few Fridays. I hope you all will enjoy them and perhaps give you a little bug to visit the Emerald Isles.

"If only wishing it mase it so" Author Unknow Wishes.

"In every walk with nature one receives far more than he seeks" Joh Muir

The day was cloudy and moist. I drove down the narrow road. I could hear waves crashing on the shores as I drove and smelled the salty ocean. The road ended in a small parking lot. The ruins of a castle stood on a bluff that looked over the ocean. I walked onto the slick rocky beach to get a better look at the castle and saw a small cave across from a fast-flowing river which made it hard to get to. I wondered if this small cave led to a secret underground chamber below the castle. Something I would not find out because of the fast-flowing river.

I walked up the road to the castle. The castle was enclosed with a fence that had signs of "danger" and "no trespassing" attached to them. Then I spotted the gate. It opened onto a small path. I walked down the path and came upon a well. A sign that read "tobar eoin" Which is Irish for John's Well. The well was surrounded by a semicircle of stone and a small stone opening that looked like it was meant for kneeling. There was a gnarly tree with its roots exposed on a small hill behind the well. All kinds of tokens were tied or placed among the roots. I felt that I needed to leave something. I had a small rock that I found during one of my adventures in Ireland. I scratched my name in Ogham, an ancient Irish druid language. (that is another story), on the rock and placed it among the roots. I then bent down to the well and cupped some of the water. The cool water dripped into the well creating ripples.

I walked back to my car. the sky was still cloudy and moist, but I had a sense of peace and hopefully the luck and blessings of an Irish wishing well.

http://www.megalithicireland.com/Minard%20Castle.html

http:ljwww.megalithicireland.com/St%20John's%20Well,%20Kilmurry,%20Kerry.htm1

What would you wish for?

The waving man

We meet many wonderful, strange, and interesting people throughout our lives. Sometimes they are in your own backyard.

"Do not neglect to show hospitality to strangers, for by doing that some have entertained angels without knowing it." Hebrews 13:2

". . . sometimes one feels freer speaking to a stranger than to people one knows. Why is that?" "Probably because a stranger sees us the way we are, not as he wishes to think we are."- Carlos Ruiz Zafon, The Shadow of the Wind

He walked down the same stretch of road from the suburbs of Reno into the city every day. He usually walked with a big walking stick, and he wore comfortable casual clothes. He waved at practically every car that passed him. I would watch him pass the convenient store I worked at every morning.

One day my friend and I were driving by when we decided to see who this man was and why did he walk this same route every day. He was a little startled when two young men pulled up in a car got out and approach him. After realizing we were harmless, we had a wonderful conversation. I do not recall what we talked about and even remember what his reasoning for walking the same route every day was. When we finished talking, he reached into this leather shoulder satchel and handed each of us a stone.

"This is a stone of Tranquility. He said to me. I felt it matches you." He handed me a smooth round, grey rock." He then handed my friend a rock as well. I do not remember what he told him what his rock was, but it must have been one that "matched" him. We both took are stones, left the "waving man" so he could continue his journey. That was the last time we talked to him. We saw him a couple of times while passing down that stretch of road, and we made sure to give a friendly wave. In which, he returned amiably.

I always wondered why "tranquility", was it because I needed it at the time or that it was a quality that I had in myself. Regardless, the reason for why this strange waving man gave me that specific stone wasn't important. It was the brief encounter that mattered.

Years later I learned who this man was. He was a bit of a celebrity and was known as "The Waver". I'm sure my friend and I were not the only ones he touched and gave stones out that "matched them". I found an article on-line about this stranger who to this day I remember that short memorable encounter. In the article it described him like this "He was committed to love and believed that the best thing we can do is share it with one another." A statement that I share.

Who was the most interesting stranger you met?

The Video Return

I worked the late shift at a 24-hour convenient store when I was a young man. You get the most interesting characters during those times.

"Where's your will to be weird?" "People are strange . . ." - Jim Morrison

No matter the circumstances that you may be going through, just push through it. -Ray Lewis

The old man came into the store around 2 in the morning. He was bleeding, bruised and his pants were torn. I recognized him as one of the "regulars". I do not recall his name. I do not even think he even mentioned his name. He usually came in to rent movies or buy snacks. Bedraggled, panting, and limping, he walked up to the counter and handed me a video.

"What happened," I said, taking the video "Let me clean that wound."

I got the first aid kit, handed him some paper towels to clean the blood. He told me his tail as I cleaned him up. "I found the video and I don't recall if it was late or not. So, to be sure I decided I should bring it back right away. So, I headed out." Now, remember It is 2 in the morning now.

"I decided to take a shortcut through the fields. I forgot that there was a fence at the end of the field, so I decided to climb it." This guy was at least 60 if not older.
"During the climb, my pants got caught on the top of the fence. I hung there for a little while. I could not get loose. I tugged and tugged until my pants ripped and the jagged top of the fence tore this cut in me. I fell to the ground and my video went flying into the dark."

"I spent about an hour trying to find it. I did not have a flashlight. I finally found it a couple of feet in the bushes. Boy! I had the dickens of a time getting it out of there." Which, I could tell by the scratches and torn clothing. I looked at the video and noticed it was not rewound, and it was a little dirty.

"How much do I owe you?" He asked.

"Nothing, you got it back on time," I said with a grin.

He was several days late, and we usually charged a rewind fee if they didn't rewind it. I sent him home with a flashlight and complimentary slurpy.

When did you help someone and what was the circumstance?

The Leather Shop

Exploring and finding the little corners of wherever you travel can be the most memorable times in your life. Dingle, Ireland is such a place.

"Standing within a peat bog in Dingle, you can't help wondering what Ireland was like before you and the other primates scrambled up upon its shores. When viewed from space, did it glow like a furry emerald within a sea of blue, the terrestrial equivalent of a massive marine plankton bloom?" We - Author: Hope Jahren

"To be a muse is to be a wonder in someone else's eyes, flaws and all." L.H. Cosway, Still Life with Strings

We drove into the touristy but quint little coastal town of Dingle. There was parking down by the docks. A tour bus lounged in its parking spots while the tourists departed and dispersed into Dingle. It was off-season there were not as many "foreigners" as there would be in the warmer summer season. We were among those foreigners, except our mode of transport was a white rental car.

My daughter, her friend, and I walked down the shoulder-to-shoulder buildings and found a pub that advertised the best fresh fish chowder. I took the bait and did indeed have the best fish chowder I have ever tasted.

We wandered around Dingle. The girls went in one direction, and I went in another. We had different interests, and the two friends wanted some time alone, without this old dad tagging along.

I found a few souvenir shops that had various Irish merchandise. I was trying to find a nice writing journal. One shop had a big selection of beautiful leather-bound journals engraved with different Irish themes. However, none had the specific theme I was looking for, one with the Celtic symbol of the tree of life.

The middle-aged shopkeeper informed me of a little leather shop down the road that may have what I am looking for.

I walked down to this white wall with blue trim shop. Two signs indicated that I found the correct place. A circular sign with the words "Uisce Saddlery Leather Workshop" hung on the corner of the store and a similar worded sign was attached to the wall over the windows.

I was greeted by two friendly Border Collies. One stood to get a pat and the other went back to its dog bed located behind the counter. A petite short haired woman wearing a leather apron looked up from a piece of leather she was looking on and greeted me.

This little leather workshop in the beautiful little coastal town of Dingle and its owner will become a memory I will always recall. The craftsmanship was top-notch. It was also a venue for local artists. It also brought inspiration to me with these short stories which I hope will be more prevalent in the future. Uisce Saddlery Leather Workshop became my Muse shop.

What was your favorite shop or place that you have been to?

Route one

I drove across the United States three times in my life. All three were with my friend Jim. The 1st time was moving out to Reno, Nevada. The 2nd was to go to Aspen, Colorado for a wedding and the third was to revisit Reno, Nevada after I moved back to Vermont.

"Traveling -it leaves you speechless, then turns you into a storyteller." -Ibn Battuta

"Travel isn't always pretty. It isn't always comfortable. Sometimes it hurts, it even breaks your heart. But that's okay. The journey changes you; it should change you. It leaves marks on your memory, on your consciousness, on your heart, and on your body. You take something with you. Hopefully, you leave something good behind." - Anthony Bourdain

During these travels, I like to meet, talk, and associate with the locals of each place that I visit. I feel that you get to know the regions much better. It also gave me an appreciation of different types of people and cultures. Even though we are one big country there are so many little pockets of different cultures within this country. Even down to little towns in the states.

Several years ago, I had an opportunity to travel on my own. I chose to go to California to visit relatives and friends. I rented a car and drove up Route One which ran up the coast of California. I started in San Diego and ended in San Francisco. During this solo adventure, I made a vlog. (I believe that is the term people use these days.) I came up with the name "Silent Storm in the Belly." My 1st entree I explain why I call it that name.

I think of those memories today, while isolated. I wonder about the places and people that I experienced on that "silent Storm in the Belly" trip. Does Maddy, the young lifeguard I met at Laguna Beach still have a job? Or does Jeff Bridges still bike around there (Yes, I almost got run over by Jeff Bridges). Do people still stop and watch the Elephant seals. I think of these things while in isolation. I am glad that they are there to recall. There are only so many shows you can watch on Netflix. During quiet times at home or driving in my car, I can access my shows in my head.

I hope to add some more shows to my "Netflix" head once this pandemic is done. I am pretty sure I will not be the only one.

Have you ever traveled alone?

Fog

Fog has long been a mysterious—and at times frightening—phenomenon throughout human history. But I've come to see it differently. For me, fog isn't something to fear, it's something to remember.

Here are a few of those memories.

"Sometimes when you lose your way in the fog, you end up in a beautiful place! Don't be afraid of getting lost!" Mehmet Murat I/don.

"Love Is a fog that burns with the first daylight of reality." Charles Bukowski.

"The truth is a fog, in which one man sees the heavenly host and the other one sees a flying elephant." Terry Pratchett

The day started unseen; my home was obscured by fog. The porch light penetrated only a few feet into the misty white air, creating halos as the light refracted off the mist. The air was moist and clung to clothes and skin. The sun is a giant dimly lit porch light hovering above the fog. I walked out into the mist and watched my dog disappear into obscurity. I hear her moving around in the distance. I close my eyes and remember.

The sound of the surf, the wind blows the white, ghostly fog around me. I smell the salty sea. It is quiet except for the waves and wind.

I stand on a cliff looking at the colorful patchwork landscape with clouds and fog nestling amongst the vibrant hills. The air is crisp and cool. It is quiet until I hear a crow's cawing echoing through the valley.

I awoke to mist. I crawl out of my tent and walk down to the lake to see the fog escaping the water like spirits moving off to the afterlife. I hear the cry of a loon echoing through the lake.

I open my eyes to find my dog is by my feet with a ball in her mouth. It is useless throwing the ball now. It would never find it. However, I picked it up anyway and threw it into the fog. I trust that she will use her other senses to locate the ball.

Your most mystical place?

Driving on the left

The flight got into Ireland at 5 am. My body registered at midnight because there is a 5-hour difference. Luckily, I managed to sleep a little on the plane. My daughter, her friend, and I got our luggage and headed to the rental cars.

"In Ireland, speed limits are more like challenges."-unknown.

"He who travels has stories to tell." - Irish proverb.

After getting the extra car insurance and the portable Wi-Fi hotspot device (Wi-Fi candy, highly recommended if you are traveling in Ireland). I sat in the car getting myself acquainted with all the controls being on the right side of the car. I paid the extra money to get an automatic. I didn't need any other distractions especially since I never drove a manual.

We drove off in our little white, packed car. Luckily the parking garage had big white arrows pointing out how to get out. However, once I got to the road, I had to switch my brain to the left instead of the right.

The girls, although tired, kept vigilance on my driving to make sure I didn't go to the right side. One of them was the navigator. Then I hit the circle! "Ok, go into it on the left...Oh no! Why are there many lanes in this circle? Which one do I choose?"

"Take the 2nd exit," said our navigator. I quickly darted across two lanes to get to the exit.

Luckily, there were not many cars on the road currently. We went through 3 or 4 of these circles, in which I managed to stay left. I have no idea if I did it properly.

Shortly after this circle madness, we were driving on a highway that looked very similar to what I am used to. The sun was just coming up. The girls settled in for a nap, now that we were safe.

5 hours later I was driving down a road where it didn't matter if I was on the right or the left because there was only "a middle". We encountered a bold deer who casually moved up the road not caring that there was a car with humans in it bearing slowly down on it.

After a couple of scratches (That extra insurance paid off!) and gasp from my passengers, my brain was now left-sided. I was used to driving left down narrow roads that sometimes-had hedges on one side and stone walls on another. Despite the challenges of driving in Ireland. I was happy to have the freedom to go wherever I wanted, even with the gasps from my passengers.

Have you ever driven in a foreign country?

Traveling with Strangers

I have traveled in the United States and in Ireland. In both countries and probably around the world, you run into strangers that are good people. It is important to trust your instincts and sometimes take some chances with strangers.

"May the road rise to meet you."-Irish proverb.

"Be afraid of nothing." -Oscar Wilder

Tears streaking down her cheeks, we embraced and kissed. I was saying goodbye to my Irish beauty, host, and friend, Helen. We did not know when we would ever meet again. I walked onto the bus and got a seat next to the window so I could wave goodbye to her one last time.

The bus was heading for Galway, then Shannon. I had three days before I was heading back to the United States, so I decided to spend the last few days on my own exploring the city of Galway. I had never been there. I planned on finding a youth hostel for the night, exploring Galway the next day, then heading to Shannon, where I would spend the night and catch my flight the next day.

I overheard two women sitting behind me on the packed bus talk about going to a youth hostel once they got to Galway. I turned to them as we were departing the bus and said I was looking for a youth hostel as well. They gladly invited me to follow them. I do not remember their names; however, one was from Germany and the other from England. As I got off the bus a young boy came up to me and asked if I needed a guide for the city. Before I could answer the two women shooed him off and told me to follow them. We all hoisted on our backpacks and headed into the city.

I followed them through a maze of streets. I trusted that they knew their way and that they were not leading me to an alley to mug me. We came to this nonchalant red door that had no sign (that I noticed). We were in a section of the city where all the buildings were attached to each other like one big wall, their facades punctuated with doors of many different colors. They knocked on the door and a man opened it. We were at the youth hostel. After paying the lodging fee and a little extra to keep our backpacks safely behind the desk, we headed up to our rooms. The women slept in one section and men in the other. I entered a bunk room with quite a few bunk beds scattered around the room. Some of the beds had stuff on them, so I climbed one up high and placed my small travel bag on it. Now, I knew why paying the extra money was prudent. There was no security.

I met my traveling companions in the common lounge later and we headed out across the street to a local pub they knew about. We entered an empty pub. Without hesitating, the two women headed through the pub and up some stairs. This is where the action was. The room was crowded. A circle of musicians was in the middle of the room jamming. Everyone was happy and loud. The two women and I found a spot. Soon the rounds were bought, and everyone was having a good time.

Any traveling and meeting stranger tales to tell?

Abba and Donegal

One of the perks of traveling to different places is experiencing the local architecture.

Ireland has amazing ruins scattered throughout the countryside. It is so common that the locals seem to not even notice them anymore.

Why did the Egyptian architect go to jail? He was caught planning a pyramid scheme.

The bus headed out of Dublin. Helen and I had comfortable seats towards the back. "Dancing Queen" played on the bus speakers. In fact, the whole Abba album played repeatedly through the several hours bus drive. The only time the bus driver stopped the music was when we crossed into Northern Ireland and an armed soldier came onto the bus to "inspect" it. Helen warned me of this ahead of time, so I wasn't startled when he walked past me in the aisle. Once the inspections finished the bus continued and "Knowing Me, Knowing You" blared on the speakers.

The day started out nicely, then clouded over. A typical Irish day in September. I woke up early from Helen's relatives' house and went for a walk. I noticed this ancient ruined keep up on the hill down the road from the house. Sights like this were scattered throughout Ireland. I navigated through the thick thistle bushes. Now, I knew why things looked like a patchwork flying into Ireland. Later I was perched on the top of this couple of centuries old ruin, looking out to the shore. I imagine that this must have been what the ancient Celts saw watching for invaders on their shores. I didn't stay up long because I was a little self-conscious about perching on an ancient building where all the locals could see me.

I plan on going back to that ruin again with my kids. I would love them to have their own experience with ancient Celtic ruins.

Have you ever visited ruins?

The Emerald Isle

Many, many years ago I went to Ireland, and this was my experience going to Ireland. I plan on going back with my family one of these days.

"Saint Patrick would have never believed how his memory would become perceived In the Emerald Isle. They do it in style with green outfits, green hats, and green sleeves."

"I once met a monk who could inspire when espousing his spiritual fire and soon, I had found He was quite profound in fact, you could call him a deep friar!"

I looked in wonder at the rich green patchwork quilt of fields below me. It was greener than Vermont on a spring day.

Now I knew why they called this beautiful land the Emerald Isle. I smiled at Dick and Sheila; the older couple who had "adopted" me during the flight from New York to Ireland. I met this couple just before boarding the flight. We bonded right off. It helped that their first names happened to be the same as my parents'.

During our conversations on the flight, they learned that I was to meet my pen pal in Dublin. However, because I was a foreigner I had to get off in Shannon. I was on the opposite side of the country from where I was to be. My adoptive parents agreed to take me as far at Mullingar, which was midway between Shannon and Dublin. I quickly went to a pay phone (this was before cell phones) and called my worried pen pal. I was supposed to be in Dublin an hour ago. I assured her that I was in Ireland, and I would make my way to Dublin.

We zoomed through the gully-like roads of the Irish landscape in the little car that Dick and Sheila had rented for their vacation and arrived in Mullingar in the early afternoon. They bought me fish and chips at a little restaurant, then sent me on my way. I walked to the bus station. However, before I got there, I decided to try something that I saw many people doing as we traveled the roads of Ireland: hitch hiking.

I put my backpack on and started down the road. I had made it a couple of miles out of Mullingar when it started to rain. Hitch hiking was unsuccessful even when I wrote "Dublin" on a piece of cardboard I found.

I walked back to the bus station, bought a ticket to Dublin, and called my pen pal again to tell her where I was. "Ride the bus until the very end; that is where I will pick you up," instructed Helen, my pen pal.

Now, those are easy instructions. The only problem is that the bus driver never said the name of any stops. He would just stop, and people would get off and on. They knew this system and I was the accidental tourist. What made matters worse was every time I asked what the stop's name was, I always got a person whose accent was so strong I didn't understand anything they said. Luckily, a bunch of school-aged kids got on the bus whose accents were much easier to understand. They were more than happy to help me out.

My new friends all suddenly got off the bus and soon the bus was empty. I figured it must be the last stop. So, I got off. I did not see Helen waiting for me. So, I found a pay phone and called her. "Oh, you got off at the second to the last stop." She gave me directions to O'Connell Street and told me to wait at the monument by the water fountain. I followed the directions and was relieved to see my beautiful dark-haired pen pal walk over to me and give me a big hug. This was the start of many other Irish adventures which I may divulge to you later.

Where do you want to go?

The Carrygerry House

Here is part two of my previous story. Since we have all been in isolation and traveling has been at a very minimal if at all, I've been thinking of my past travel adventures.

"Airports are gonna go from being the meanest place to be to the nicest once we're allowed to fly again. Check my bag? Go ahead. Screaming baby? Sit right next to me, buddy."

"Riddle: What travels around the world but stays in one corner? Answer: A stamp!"

The Irish countryside swept past me as I rode the bus down to Shannon, Ireland. The sun was setting as the bus arrived at the bus depot. The transportation system in Ireland was cheap and efficient. The only drawback was the bus driver hardly ever announced which stop was which. I guess everyone knew where they were going, except for us foreigners.

The day before, I had spent time in Galway, exploring, and listening to great music; there happened to be a music festival when I was there. My new, brief friends from England and Germany went their own way just before my explorations. I was on my own.

In Shannon, I had to find a place to stay for one night before I headed back home. I hired a taxi and asked the cab driver to take me to the airport hotel. We drove to this very fancy hotel. During the drive, he informed me how fancy the hotel was. Dignitaries from all around the world stayed there. I still wanted to at least check it out. He offered to wait for me while I checked it out.

I walked into the grand entryway of the hotel bedraggled from traveling for a few days. Several well-dressed people lingered in the lobby. A couple glanced up at me. I ignored them and walked towards the desk. The concierge was busy talking to a traditionally dressed African man at the desk. I looked around, waited for a few minutes, then walked out. I was a little out of place here and the price was a little steep for me.

We drove to the other side of the airport. The cab driver advised me that there was a small B&B called <u>Carrygerry Country House</u>. on the other side of the airport, that would be more suitable for me.

The driver asked me when my flight was leaving. I told him. He offered to pick me up and take me to the airport the next day. I gave him a big tip and thanked him.

I was greeted by a middle-aged woman, owner of the spacious and elegant B&B (not as ostentatious as the hotel). I paid for my room, and she took me up to a good-sized bedroom with its own bathroom. She asked if I would be dining tonight. I said I would. She informed me, when I was ready, to go down to the sitting room. Someone would get me when dinner was ready. I took much needed shower, put on my best clothes, and headed down to the sitting room. Later. I sat by myself at a big, elegantly arranged table. A few well-dressed families were sitting at nearby tables. I heard several different languages. I was underdressed compared to everyone else. Even the kids had little suits and dresses on!

I felt a little out of place. I thought to myself. "OK, according to my dad, we come from Irish royalty (a boast that I think every Irishman claims). I sat up a little straighter, looking down at the formally arranged cutlery. "OK. I think the salad fork is on the outside," I thought to myself. I then enjoyed a 4-course meal while listening to the rain patter against the glass roof of the dining room.

Favorite place you stayed at when you traveled?

Strangers and Friends

There are good people out there. I have witnessed them. I met them. I have interacted with them. I have driven across the United States 3 times. I have met many people and seen many United States cultures. Here is but one example of a good person.

Why did the librarian get kicked off the plane? Because it was too booked.

It was a long drive, and it was getting late. Jim and I had just gotten into the outskirts of Madison, Wisconsin (which happens to be where my friend Rob settled down many years later). It was the summer of 1989.

We stopped at one of those 24-hour convenience stores. We were tired and needed to find a hotel or camping park for the night. While we were in the store, we got into a conversation with the young store clerk. She told us that she was watching a professor's house in downtown Madison. She would not be getting home until after her shift, which got done at 7:30 am. She offered that we could stay there for the night. We must have impressed her, or she was just a kind, trusting soul.

I do not know why we said yes. I guess we were impressed by her genuine gesture. As a token of trust, Jim gave her his driver's license. We set off to find this house.

Following her directions (this was before cell phones and Google maps). We drove through nice neighborhoods. Madison was a university city so there were many educational professionals who lived in nice houses and neighborhoods. We found out later that Madison in general is a nice place to live. It was one of the cleanest capitals I have been to.

We finally pulled into the driveway of a brick, colonial style house. Unlocked the door with the key the clerk gave us and were met by two friendly cats. We chose to sleep on the two couches that were in the living room. However, before we settled in for the night, we noticed that there was very little food in the cabinets. We happened to have a supply of canned goods and other non-perishable food for our travels. So, we stocked up her cabinets.

After a night with a cat sleeping on my face, we were woken up by the clerk coming in from her shift. She had brought some coffee home with her from her store. So, we sat on the couches and drank our coffees and chatted a little. We found out that she was an artist, and she showed us some of the pictures that she had penciled. She had quite a few. After looking through them she asked us to pick one out. I picked one of a fat friendly looking dragon. "It's yours." We both were still astonished by the generosity of this young artist. I asked her if she wouldn't mind signing it. So, she wrote a little poem on my fat little dragon and signed it.

I still have a fat little dragon. It is tucked away somewhere in storage. I plan on searching for it and putting it up in my new (well, 3 years old) home.

Remember, strangers are only friends that you haven't met yet.

Have you ever met a stranger who impacted your life?

Sea Caves

It was a misty cool day, typical of Ireland during this time of the year. I was winding through the narrow roads of The Ring of Beara in County Cork. My drive was slow because of the views; narrow roads and I still got used to driving on the left side of the road. I rounded a bend and had to pull over. A beautiful rainbow filtered down through the mist settling on the top of a nearby mountain. I had to take a picture.

"To be Irish to stand tall as the cliffs with the soul as deep as the ocean" Irish Proverb

It was like Ireland was asking me to take a picture because this was my third rainbow on my Ring of Beara tour. I had to comply with this subtle demand.

Sometimes it was hard to believe that I was on a major tourist attraction drive. The road was so narrow that there was no way a bus would make it through. At one point it looked like you were driving onto a farm, however, the road turned and went around the farm.

My final destination was Cuas Pier Sea Caves. I read about them on a website. Luckily, I had the directions on my Google maps. The Irish-voiced Google assistant (I had to change the accent) directed me faithfully through the winding, narrow roads of Ireland.

My Irish assistant informed me that I had to turn right when I got to the end of the road. A small country store that acted as the post office was on the corner. I stopped to get petrol and saw how close I was to the caves. I walked into the all-in-one store, paid for the petrol, and got some gum. The clerk/post person was more than happy to let me know how close I was to the caves. I listened patiently to her directions.

Moments later with the assistance of both of my Irish assistants I was parked at the rough parking lot that ended near the caves. It was the only place to go. There was a sign depicting a car driving off the pier with a cross through it. I was the only one there.

The day was still misty and cool, which added to the magical feeling of the caves. I walked into the caves as far as I could without getting too wet. Waves crashed in the cave sounding like thunder. I dared not go too far into the cave because I didn't want to get caught off guard by the high tide.

I walked up the muddy and narrow path above the caves. I came to the rocky shores on the other side and looked out into the vast ocean. My jacket fluttered with the strong sea wind. I could smell the salty ocean as I looked east out into the vast ocean. I sighed and smiled. I was looking home. I also felt like I was home.

Where is your favorite place to be in nature?

Shawn O'Neil is a lifelong Vermonter and father of three, with roots that stretch all the way back to Ireland—which he loves to visit. He's worked as a clerk, librarian, and IT helpdesk technician, but what he really loves is writing stories, telling them, and helping other people tell theirs.

Years ago, he started a little tradition called "Pundays"—every Friday he'd send a pun, a joke, or a quote to a few coworkers. Just something to make folks smile (or roll their eyes) after a long week. When the world shut down in 2020, and everything felt a little uncertain, he decided to up his game. He started adding short stories to the Pundays. One story led to another, and before long, he was sharing them across Vermont and working on this book.

Scéal Do Bheatha is part personal storytelling, part invitation—for you to reflect, remember, and maybe even write your own.

www.ingramcontent.com/pod-product-compliance
Lightning Source LLC
Chambersburg PA
CBHW080345300426
44110CB00019B/2511